Mediterranean Modern

Dominic Bradbury

To Florence

With thanks to Lucas Dietrich, Elain McAlpine, Aaron Hayden, Cat Green and all at Thames & Hudson and to Jonathan Pegg at Curtis Brown, Eugeni Pons and Faith Bradbury. Thanks also to all of the architects – and their clients – who have assisted in the development of this book.

Designed by Broadbase

Photo credits: 1, 4 (bottom), 7, 170-183 Jean-Luc Laloux; 2-3, 30-37 Hisao Suzuki; 4 (top), 10, 11, 18-29, 38-47, 48-55, 62-71, 102-109, 110-112, 114, 115 (bottom), 116-118, 120-129, 138-145, 146-153, 154-161, 204-213, 234-243, 256 Eugeni Pons; 4 (middle), 13, 90-101 Dan Glasser; 8, 192-203 © Peter Cook/VIEW; 14, 72-79 Roland Halbe Fotografie; 17, 214-223 Serge Demailly; 56-61 Pietro Savorelli; 80-89 Eugeni Pons/RBA; 113, 115 (top), 119 Julia Klimi; 130-137 Mayte Piera; 162-169 © Christian Michel/VIEW; 184-186, 190, 191 (bottom) Katerina Tsigarida Architects; 188, 189 (top), 191 (top) Yiorgis Gerolympos; 189 (bottom) Erieta Attali; 224-233 Cemal Emden; 244-253 Alberto Muciaccia

First published in the United Kingdom in 2006 by
Thames & Hudson Ltd, 181A High Holborn, London WC1V 7QX

www.thamesandhudson.com

British Library Cataloguing-in-Publication Data

A catalogue record for this book is available from the British Library

ISBN-13: 978-0-500-34227-5
ISBN-10: 0-500-34227-X

Printed and bound in China by Everbest Printing Co Ltd

Sky

Earth

Sea

Introduction

It is a crossroads, a border zone, a trade route, a pleasure ground. It is a great cradle of culture and the birthplace of Western architecture. But the Mediterranean is also a place of intense and profound cross-pollination with the vibrant influences of myriad past cultures – Greek, Roman, Ottoman, Moorish – feeding and informing the rich state of the present and the future.

For centuries, the whole of Europe has been drawn to the Mediterranean, seeing within its coastal lands countless possibilities and opportunities. Above all, it has been and still is a place of escapism. The legacy of the Grand Tour remains in the eternal desire to travel the Mediterranean in search of landscape, history, sun, and seduction, and to drink in experience and the flavours of the sea. This desire is not simply a European dream anymore, but a more international aspiration, drawing incomers from around the world.

We are still drawn to the enticements of the corniche, to the glamour and exotic associations of the celebrated Mediterranean tourist stops of Monaco, Nice, Tangier, Barcelona, and the Amalfi Coast. We are also constantly seduced by the delightful simplicity of life and architecture in smaller communities and island retreats like the Aeolian Islands, Corsica, Malta, Capri, Santorini, and others.

No wonder that the idea of a Mediterranean home has a particular allure. The traditional notion of Mediterranean living is suffused with simplicity, an openness to landscape and the sea, and with that particular erosion of divisions between indoor and outdoor space, as well as an emphasis on texture, organic and sea-blown colours, and solid, natural materials. Today a new breed of architects have taken these traditional associations and reinvented them in the light of the Modernist example, designing contemporary homes infused with and informed by the past,

A view across the cactus gardens on the rooftops of a section of Can Helena, a house in the Balearic Islands designed by Belgian architect Bruno Erpicum.

The traditional notion of Mediterranean living is suffused with simplicity, an embracing of landscape and sea...

Sun loungers on the raised pool and terrace at the Villa Fleurie in the south of
France, designed by Pascal and Francine Goujon. A wall of growing flowers coats
the lower level of the building, softening its mark on the landscape.

but also innovative and woven through with new technology and engineering.

The best of modern Mediterranean architecture takes account of context, landscape, and sustainability, drawing on local traditions and vernacular styles, while still creating highly original buildings. This is particularly true of the contemporary single-family home, in which architects like Alberto Campo Baeza, Carlos Ferrater, Bruno Erpicum, and Rudy Ricciotti have pushed away from pastiche and developed a new wave of houses that respond to their settings and sites in unique but sensitive ways.

In a fascinating combination of old and new, tradition and modernity, architects such as Studio K.O., Vincenzo Melluso, Arturo Frediani, and others have been reinterpreting traditional materials like stone and *pisé* in original modern homes, grounded in landscape and history. The same is true of form and structure, in which advanced engineering on the one hand, and radically reassessing the dictates of climate on the other, have liberated the outline of the home and sent it off in many different directions. Yet these are not alien interventions, but intricate, one-off buildings born of an understanding of Mediterranean culture and an awareness of the landscapes that bring them and their clients to these settings in the first instance.

These are homes born of respect for the environment and the landscape, as well as for the fashionable yet vital issue of sustainability. They are not high-volume developments pushing themselves upon the land, but specific solutions to a particular set of challenges and demands. They also sit within the context of a number of revolutionary and inspirational 20th-century Modernist houses, classics of their time that are associated with parts of the Mediterranean.

There is a sense in which the Mediterranean coast has long been associated with experimental and innovative architecture, and this is especially true of the 20th century. One thinks of Antoni Gaudí's extraordinary inventiveness, centred upon Barcelona, with its powerful mix of Moorish and Gothic richness and Art Nouveau extravagance. At another extreme, one might mention Egyptian architect Hassan Fathy and his pioneering work in re-establishing the importance of vernacular influences in Modernist architecture. His work, like that of Luis Barragán in Mexico, has helped to reassert the value of traditional materials, like adobe or *pisé*, in contemporary forms and structures, and to encourage a younger generation of architects to make similar journeys of exploration.

Then there are other, more individual Modernist statements. Eileen Gray's E-1027 villa at Roquebrune-Cap-Martin, near Monte Carlo in the south of France, has been described as the

first truly Modernist vacation home. Painted in white and overlooking the sea with Monaco in the distance, it was a crisp ocean liner moored on the hillside, still a revolutionary statement amid the mock Provençal architecture that dominates the region.

Alongside, Le Corbusier built a small wooden cabin for himself and his wife – a very different kind of statement from Gray's E-1027, or indeed from any of his own landmark buildings. Le Corbusier simply loved the town and the sea, and was, arguably, jealous of Gray's achievement.

The contrast between sections of glass and a coat of textured granite slabs adds drama to this house in Pozuelo de Alarcón, Spain, by architects Vicens & Ramos.

His cabin, and the modest restaurant he designed next door, were very simple, basic buildings, little more than traditional wooden cabins, although filled with space-saving ideas and the architect's own painted murals. Both Gray and Le Corbusier took inspiration from this coastal spot and from the calming influence of the Mediterranean. Le Corbusier built himself an even simpler work studio nearby, where he would draw and paint with an open window to the sea. His grave now stands in the cemetery above Roquebrune-Cap-Martin, still facing the open waters.

Like E-1027, Adalberto Libera's Casa Malaparte on the island of Capri has become another iconic example of the great Modernist, Mediterranean villa. Built for the writer Curzio Malaparte and completed in 1941, the house sits alone at the tip of a small rocky peninsula reaching out into the sea. Also ship-like, yet painted terracotta, it appears deeply embedded in its extraordinary site, with a dramatic and distinctive series of tapering steps leading to a rooftop terrace. Modest openings in the sides of the building frame extraordinary views of the ocean below in this most romantic and theatrical of houses. Here Malaparte could write in isolation, surrounded by raw nature

This ideal of taking inspiration from a particular sense of place, from a particular response to the landscape and the seascape, is certainly one explanation for the wealth of architecture in parts of the Mediterranean. Certain architects came from far and wide to drink in the possibilities of the coast, to work and to build. There is Antti Lovag, for instance, the Finnish architect who settled on the Côte d'Azur and

Sections of Casa M-Lidia were prefabricated and then assembled on site to keep costs down. Situated near Montagut, in Catalonia, the house was designed by RCR Arquitectes

designed a series of ground-breaking zoomorphic 'bubble houses', using a series of interconnected concrete pods. The most famous of these is Pierre Cardin's Palais Bulles, built by Lovag in the 1970s, near Cannes.

Danish architect Jørn Utzon, designer of the Sydney Opera House, also moved to the Mediterranean in the 1970s, and built a house for himself and his wife in Majorca, on the outskirts of a small village with views out across the sea. He later handed the house over to his grown-up children and decided to build a new home in the mid-1990s on a rural mountainside site, employing local materials and Balearic vernacular influences.

Such migration has further enriched and pollinated the architecture of the Mediterranean and can be seen more and more today, with architects less constrained by geography and bureaucracy and working further afield. Belgian architect Bruno Erpicum (page 172), for example, has built his best-known work in the Balearics, but remains based in Brussels. French architects Studio K.O. are based in Paris, yet are designing and building some striking houses in Morocco.

Others, however, prefer to concentrate on a particular region that they know well and feel they understand intimately, using this detailed understanding to perfect their work within a smaller enclave, while being no less innovative in their thinking. Ramón Vilalta, Rafael Aranda and Carmen Pigem of RCR Arquitectes (page 48), for instance, have made a reputation for themselves with a series of original houses and projects in the particular region of Catalonia where they grew up and to which they returned after their architectural studies to found their practice. The work of Marc Barani (page 214), who is based in Nice, is largely local to the region (including the restoration of Le Corbusier's cabin at Cap Martin), yet has an extraordinary range and diversity within it.

Indeed, diversity is a hallmark of the architecture of the Mediterranean. As we have said, this is a region in which a mass of disparate influences collide and combine, and even within the context of the broadly neo-Modernist houses that dominate this book there is a wide range of ideas and invention. Many of these projects sit within a number of frameworks: historical, cultural, regional, as well as that of Modernist architecture itself. They take account of regional differences and vernacular elements, drawing upon a design heritage and spectrum of materials particular to that area and its landscape.

In North Africa, for instance, the legacy of architects such as Hassan Fathy is seen in the work of a new generation of architects, who are rediscovering techniques like *pisé* and *tadelakt* in striking contemporary buildings. One sees this particularly in Morocco, where an influx of wealth

Designed by French practice Studio K.O.,
Villa D. is an organic, contemporary home
made of sun-baked earthen bricks that
sits naturally within the desert landscape
at the foot of the Atlas mountains.

Casa Martemar in Málaga, by Antón Garcia-Abríl, opens itself up to the sea while presenting its largely closed flanks to the nearby houses on either side. The design of the house balances the need for privacy and the need for openness to the light and the views.

and the demand for vacation homes have provided patronage for architects such as Elie Mouyal, Charles Boccara, and others. Studio K.O's Villa D. (page 92), near Marrakech, is a powerful evolution of this fusion of traditional techniques with modern forms and contemporary layouts. The earthen house emerges from the scorched earth like a kasbah or farm compound, but is essentially contemporary in every respect. While parts of Marrakech, Casablanca, and Rabat are crippled by mass developments that have little to do with the design heritage of North Africa, homes such as Villa D., with their use of familiar techniques and materials, feel as though they belong to the region, while radically evolving the language and vocabulary of the local architecture.

One sees this contrast between the architecture of hope and that of paucity, between optimistic sensitivity and opportunistic overdevelopment, in other parts of the Mediterranean as well. Spain, in particular,

has famously experienced mass urbanization across the Costa del Sol and other coastal strips. Much of this building has been of poor quality and limited aesthetic merit, with little sense of balance between building scale and amenity space, and between population influx and the demand on resources, particularly water.

But having said that, Spain as a whole has an extraordinarily vibrant architectural scene at present, with many of the country's architects making their impact felt upon the world stage. Around Barcelona especially, with its innovative new homes and buildings, the architectural community is very strong. Even in places like Málaga, renowned for its building boom, one sees rays of hope in projects like Antón Garcia Abríl's Casa Martemar (page 72), which forges its own place and aesthetic power within the confines of a crowded and expanding city.

Overall, there are obvious concerns about the way mass development in certain Mediterranean tourist hot spots is changing the character of such places, and threatening the very beauty which first attracted visitors to the area. The pace of development in places like the Costa del Sol, Anatolia, Corfu, Casablanca, or Tunis, for example, appears to be unsustainable. Some local governments have begun to introduce tighter controls upon development in an attempt to preserve a sense of balance between landscape and housing, and between resources and demand, before the essential character of the area is destroyed.

But there is hope in the way that some parts of the Mediterranean are able to limit development, regain balance, and reinvent themselves. The Balearics, for instance, have been able to remarket themselves less as a tourist destination, and more as a place of culture, high-end homes, and exclusive ports of call.

Certainly, one feels far more optimistic about the future when considering the Mediterranean houses in these pages and the work of their architects. They prove that there is still an exciting vibrancy to the region, and a great deal of imagination at play. These are architects who are producing some powerful buildings, but are also dealing with issues like sustainability and contextual sensitivity. They have a respect for landscape and setting, and for materials which suit a particular place and climate. They are increasingly designing houses that can be used

all year round, rather than a few months out of the year, and that will stand the test of time, accepting their responsibilty in providing a model for responsible development.

Like the houses of the past, modern Mediterranean homes adopt familiar ideas like terraces and loggias, along with a certain rugged simplicity and rawness that suits the sun and the sea air. But they are also high-tech, exquisitely engineered contemporary structures that employ radical structural elements in order to experiment with form, line, and perspective. They are proof, if proof was needed, that the Mediterranean home is evolving, and that Mediterranean style is not simply about pastiche.

In some parts of the world, a 'Mediterranean home' still stands as lazy estate-agency shorthand for mock pastiche – a neoclassical villa with loggias and balconies, coated in stucco and painted white. The breadth of contemporary architecture in the region suggests that there is so much more to Mediterranean style, and that the area continues to be a place of change, excitement, diversity, and innovation, and that it cannot help but attract both architects and homemakers alike. The Mediterranean remains a region of countless possibilities and epic drama.

Overlooking the seascapes of the Côte d'Azur, this family villa designed by Marc Barani features a dramatic living room with a cantilevered concrete roof and retractable glass walls.

Modern Mediterranean homes are born of respect for the environment and the landscape, as well as the fashionable yet vital issue of sustainability.

sky

Slabs of roughly cut grey-white granite form a textured skin on the outside of the building, anchored onto a steel frame. Simple, hard landscaping and the character of the existing trees form a suitably rugged context.

Vicens & Ramos

CASA LAS ENCINAS

Pozuelo de Alarcón, Madrid

With its coat of granite and glass, this house near the Sierra de Guadarrama mountains is characterized by contemporary grandeur.

The textured granite that coats this house in Pozuelo de Alarcón lends the appearance of age and substance, seriousness and weight.

The work of Vicens & Ramos is distinguished by a certain monumentality. One sees this in such public structures as their Faculty Building in Pamplona (2001), a series of bold, concrete-faced cubes, punctured and opening up to the light. But one also sees it in domestic projects like their house in Las Matas, near Madrid, another large-scale conglomeration of interlocking geometric structures, faced in concrete and stained to an organic colour with iron sulphate, flanked in slabs of rusting steel.

This combination of organic materials and colours, and a pronounced mathematical or highly artificial composition, also characterizes the drama of Ignacio Vicens and José Antonio Ramos's house in suburban Pozuelo de Alarcón. Here we have a large eight-bedroomed family home of over 2,000 square metres, sitting within a generous, sloping site of trees and grassland. The steel frame of this cuboid building has been faced with grey granite slabs, between 7 and 12 centimetres thick, which give the overall impression of vast solidity, despite the fact that the outline of the house has been cut by horizontal and vertical incisions to form penetrating lightwells.

The roughly scored and textured granite coat, not dissimilar to the coating used to similar effect by Antón Garcia-Abríl on his Music Studies Centre at Santiago de Compostela (2002), gives the appearance of age, substance, and durability. Sitting among the trees and planting, its presence is almost temple-like in its sense of seriousness and weight.

Essentially, the building is over three floors, with an indoor swimming pool complemented by an outdoor pool and water features that contrast with the epic solidity of some of the house's retaining walls. The basement level, accessed via a long ramp, is partly buried in the hillside and holds garaging and service rooms, as well as a pool and sunken courtyard to one side. The ground floor is principally given over to a series of key living spaces, although volumes here and on the first floor vary with the inclusion of double-height rooms and skylights, making for a journey of spatial surprises throughout the building.

Opposite The house and its slabs of glazing have been likened to a geode, a stone formation with crystalline features. Retaining walls and exterior features employ the same granite coating.

Ground-floor plan

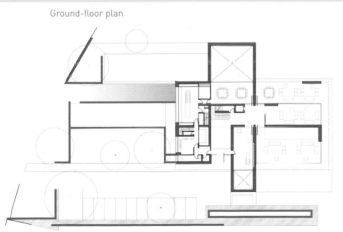

First-floor plan

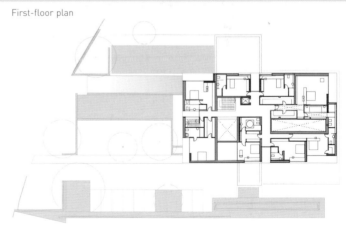

Below and opposite The three-storey house is arranged in a complex spatial formation, with a number of double-height spaces that bring a sense of drama and generosity to the building, particularly to the main living areas on the ground floor. It is also an exercise in light, with multiple light sources formed by windows at various levels and additional skylights.

Above The rough exterior texture is created during the process of extracting the stone itself. Often a smooth-cut plane would be presented to the outside, yet here the fact that the stone is irregular adds vital character to the house.

There is great generosity of space and fluidity to the main living areas, with a choice of enclosed and semi-enclosed rooms, including a furnished loggia tucked into the overall outline of the house, opening out onto terraces and gardens. Sheets of glazing allow light to flood into these key spaces, some of which are enriched by built-in furnishings, including a double-height bookcase to one side of the main living room, with its higher shelves accessed by a dedicated stairway.

At first-floor level, a series of openings and balconies within the cuboid outline bring extra light into the heart of the house, and allow occupants to benefit from views across the landscape. The house is actually placed at a low point on the site, close to the nearby access road, to create more privacy and to avoid being exposed to the neighbours, while also allowing shrubbery and planting across the rest of the plot. Thus, trees and greenery, as well as the pool, are spread out before the stone-clad home and its occupants.

Above, left and right Accessed by a series of cantilevered steps set into the rear wall, the built-in bookcase to the rear of the sitting room forms a powerful presence and is a feature in itself. Additional light filters down through this double-height section, which is pushed into the floor above.

Right The palette of materials and colours is restrained throughout the house, lending it cohesion, while the sense of perspective and drama is enhanced by the mathematical precision and detailing of every structural element.

Above and right Bathrooms and bedrooms are located on the top floor, with living spaces and the kitchen at ground level. The kitchen is oriented around a long, slim central island that also doubles as a breakfast bar.

Left and opposite, above The outdoor pool and water features complement the indoor pool in the lower level of the house. Elements such as decking and pathways are purposefully raw in flavour to reflect the building, while established trees and planting form an elegant natural backdrop and add shade and privacy.

Opposite, below Sections of the house seek to dissolve the boundaries between inside and out. Here we see the summer seating and dining area, which sits within the building's main outline, yet is partly open to the garden. The space is more than a porch or veranda, and is rather an intrinsic, sheltered part of the house with direct connections to the outdoors. Such transparency and fluidity contrast effectively with the house's monumental and enclosed stone-clad elements.

West elevation

South elevation

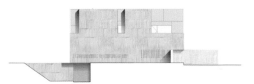

The front of the building opens out onto an elongated porch and a large limestone terrace. Metallic shutters can screen the banks of sliding-glass doors when privacy demands.

Alberto Campo Baeza

CASA ASENCIO

Chiclana, Cádiz

Deceptively simple, this flawless home delights in vibrant contrasts between openness and enclosure, light and shade.

The outward simplicity of the public face of Casa Asencio, by Alberto Campo Baeza, belies the spatial complexity within this crisp Andalusian haven. Like so much of Campo Baeza's work, the house offers a series of contrasts, between openness and enclosure, anonymity and exposure, solidity and transparency. Most importantly, it is designed around the movement, flow and availability of natural light, to the point that Campo Baeza describes light as the primary material with which the building has been pieced together, dubbing it a 'box of light and shade'.

Casa Asencio, not far from the great port city Cádiz and the gates of the Mediterranean, was commissioned by a cultivated couple who granted their architect a great deal of freedom in creating something original within an area dominated by undistinguished pastiche housing. The site of the house borders a golf club, with views of the soft undulations and greenery of the course itself.

To the nearby access road and neighbouring houses, the rear of Casa Asencio is designed as a series of tall, white walls that enclose the building and maximize privacy. But the front elevation of the house is very different, with banks of sliding-glass doors, sheltered by a porch and opening up onto the garden and the golf course beyond, and the flexibility of a metallic screen that can drop down in front of the sheets of glazing should further privacy be required. From the front of the house, a large limestone patio, together with a modest water pool, extends outwards into the garden and reflects the proportions of the house itself, maximizing the strength of architectural line and perspective, but also creating a neat hinterland between house and garden.

In many ways this formation, complete with enclosed patios to the side, echoes the success of the architect's Casa Gaspar (1991), a walled house in an orange grove in the same part of Spain.

Side section

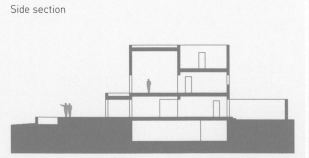

Front section

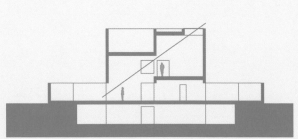

Above, left A view from the desk in the mezzanine library through the windows to the golf-course landscape. The library forms part of a volumetric journey, overlooking the double-height living spaces below.

Above, right The simple terrace forms an echo of the main building; its outline matches the footprint of the house itself. Windows are simple openings that frame the view out across the gardens and golf course.

Ground-floor plan

First-floor plan

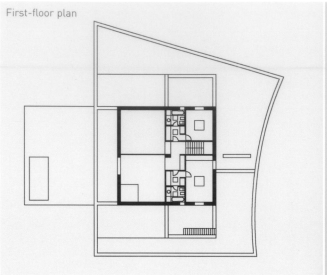

Here, too, there is a purity and simplicity to the white walls and courtyards, with an emphasis on line and detailing and a reduction of superfluity; not so much minimalism as 'essentiality', which reduces unnecessary distraction to bring the beauty of the space itself into sharp focus.

Yet in spatial terms Casa Asencio is the more complex and adventurous of the two projects, given the internal arrangement of the house in which the box-like proportions of its shell are broken down into a series of dramatic spaces of different heights and volumes. The more open living spaces feed out to the front of the house, while a mezzanine library also overlooks the golf course. The private areas of the house – bedrooms and bathrooms – are positioned to the more enclosed rear aspect. Windows that

are punctured into the framework at first-floor level offer further glimpses of the landscape and the sea, while allowing, together with a large skylight, diagonal shafts of light to illuminate the interiors.

Within the chalk-faced simplicity of Casa Asencio there are debts to Modernist influences, from Luis Barragán to Mies van der Rohe. But the house also acknowledges its ties to Andalusian tradition, updating and reinventing familiar regional ideas. 'It is very Andalusian in its deepest sense,' says Campo Baeza, 'not only in the white walls and simple construction, but also in the height of the spaces and the patios protecting the house. It appears as though the house has always been there, long before the housing developments arrived.'

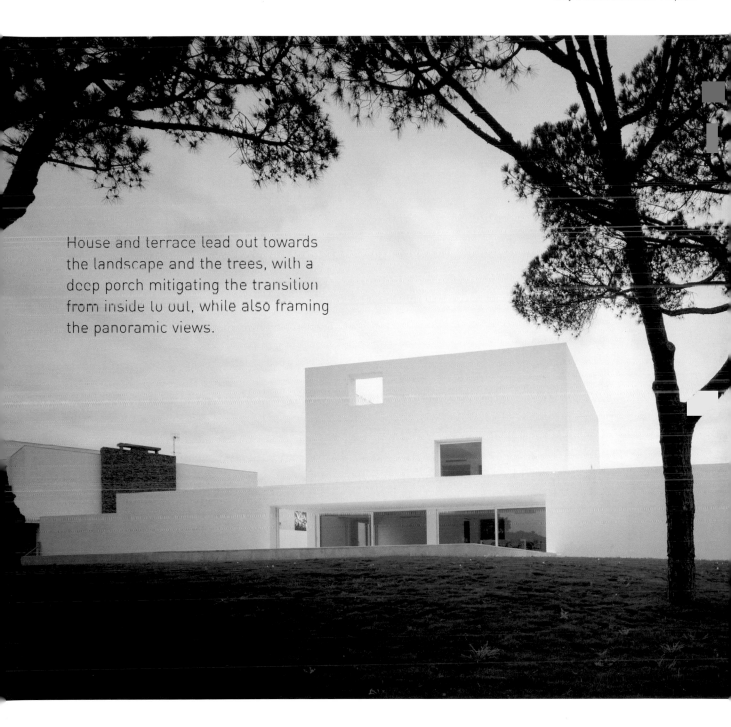

House and terrace lead out towards
the landscape and the trees, with a
deep porch mitigating the transition
from inside to out, while also framing
the panoramic views.

Above The rear of the building is the more private face of the house, with a driveway entrance to one side, feeding into the compound, and large walls protecting it from the access road. The window openings are modest and the detailing crisp.

Above, right Sliding-glass doors open from the dining area to the porch and terrace, framing views of the trees and grassland and protecting the house from the full intensity of the sun.

Right Bathrooms also involve a play on light, with skylights and modest window openings. The palette of materials is typically restrained, with an emphasis on precise detailing.

Opposite A skylight at the top of the house throws light down to the mezzanine library and the main living spaces below. A dining area is tucked underneath the library, although spaces are lightly divided in a fluid floor plan.

The house is pushed into the sloping site, opening up on three levels towards views of woodland to the south. The bottom level leads out to the garden and pool.

BFP Architectes

FONTPINEDA HOUSE

Fontpineda, Pallejà

Crimson walls and layers of travertine cladding add drama to this contemporary family home, built into the hillside.

Mediterranean architecture, like that of Latin America, has a particular colour palette. There are the earthy terracottas, reds, and pinks inspired by the landscape, and the turquoise and aquamarine shades of the sea. Contemporary architects have often opted for the safety of white houses, echoing the traditional whitewash used across the Mediterranean to reflect the sun. But other designers, including BFP Architectes, are not afraid to experiment with different tones and textures, following the enduring inspiration of Luis Barragán and Ricardo Legoretta, who proved beyond doubt that colour has a definite place within the language of Modernism.

With their house in the village of Fontpineda, about 24 kilometres outside Barcelona, BFP (namely Pablo Beltrán, Alfonso Fernández and Robin Perna) have used contrasting exterior coatings to create zones of texture and colour. Sections of the building are coated in crimson-painted concrete, while other areas are layered with horizontally placed slabs of travertine. Inside are floors in San Vicente stone and large elements of built-in furniture, such as bookcases, in timber. Repeated textural contrasts between natural and artificial materials occur both inside and out, although overall there is also restraint and continuity over the house's three floors.

'Each project is a creative challenge,' says Beltrán, 'and each house has its own personality.

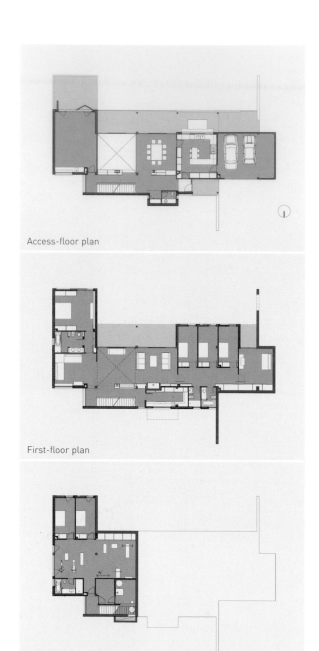

Access-floor plan

First-floor plan

Second-floor plan

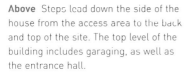

Above Steps lead down the side of the house from the access area to the back and top of the site. The top level of the building includes garaging, as well as the entrance hall.

Above, right The sides of the building are brightened by banks of crimson on cement, while windows are discreetly positioned to protect the house from its nearby neighbours.

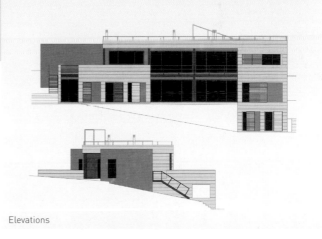

Elevations

The infinity pool makes the most of the hillside location and the spectacular views of the surrounding countryside. The retaining walls are in travertine to tie in with the house itself, while blue mosaic coats the base of the pool.

The idea here is to contrast the red walls and the travertine within abstract and clean volumes. Texture is also important, with the uniformity of the walls and the travertine's irregular surface.'

The house is located in an urban community, in close proximity to its neighbours, within a sloping site with views across forestry to the south. To maximize privacy, the side elevations are largely closed, with the house opening up to the strong southern aspect in a façade with three levels of glazing, partly recessed, and terracing or balconies. Built into the slope, the house is accessed from the top level, complete with garaging, with an access road directly behind. This level also contains the kitchen and dining area, overlooking a double-height living room below, along with a large painting studio. The middle floor forms the primary living space, with an open-plan living room leading to a large terrace, and a triptych of single bedrooms to one side and a master suite to the other. The lower ground-floor level, on a much smaller footprint, holds a gym and two further bedrooms, and leads out to the infinity pool in the garden.

Within other projects, such as BFP Architectes' house at Torrevieja, near Alicante (1998–2000), we have similar drama born of contrasts in material and colour within strong, geometric patterns. They suggest many alternatives to the simplicity of the glass or whitewashed Miesian cube that now forms such a familiar statement.

Below The mid- and upper levels include shaded terraces within the overall outline of the building, and the rocky landscaping contrasts with the crisply cut stone used to coat the house itself.

Left Boundary walls are also clad in stone, set in horizontal strips. Slim access ways run down either side of the house, which is positioned close to neighbouring buildings, hence the limited number of openings to the side elevations.

Above The top levels of the house feature the kitchen and dining area, as well as garaging and a studio. A long and partially shaded balcony offers an alternative outdoor eating area with close access to the kitchen.

Opposite The sloping site opens out into forestry below, with the pool appearing to spill over the edge. Landscaping is simple, providing a modest plateau of lawn that merges into a sea of woodland greenery.

Left The westernmost flank of the building
consists of three levels, with a gym and
guestrooms on the lowest level opening out
onto the front garden and swimming pool.

Above and opposite, above left The sitting
room has banks of glazing opening onto
a partially sheltered terrace, whereas the
balcony of the mezzanine dining area allows
light to pass freely between the two areas.

Left Bedrooms are positioned at either side of
the house, with key living spaces in between.
All bedrooms have direct access to the garden,
while the balcony and terrace form shaded
seating areas

Above Skylights bring light down into the
heart of the building, which features built-in
elements such as the bookcases to one side
of the sitting room, and stone floors.

With glass-and-metal grill walls around a system of concrete supports, Casa M-Lidia was built in sections on the factory floor to keep costs down for young clients seeking a new home.

RCR Arquitectes

CASA M-LIDIA
Montagut, Girona

Partly prefabricated, this affordable version of the contemporary country house forms a belvedere in a rural landscape.

The work of RCR Arquitectes is rooted in a particular part of Spain, a rural area surrounding the Catalan town of Olot, where its three principals grew up and to which they returned to found their practice after studying in Barcelona. Yet there is nothing parochial or narrow-minded about their work, which draws upon a large range of influences and then beds the results in very specific responses to site and landscape. 'We know our place and we need our peace to do our work, to think,' architect Ramón Vilalta has said. 'We work with the landscape. Everything comes from an abstract synthesis of the surroundings.'

A recent series of houses in the region by Vilalta and his partners, Rafael Aranda and Carmen Pigem, has drawn international attention for the originality of the trio's work, their sensitivity to site, and the detail of execution. Many of the projects were conceived not simply as houses, but as belvederes, capturing and framing this rugged, hill-specked countryside where the River Fluvia carves its way through the valleys, through Olot itself, and down to the Mediterranean. There is the Panoramic House (1999), in Olot, and the House for an Ironmonger and a Hairdresser (2001), in Canya, both of which, although quite distinct in terms of materials and arrangement, have the common Miesian quality of the rectangular, glass-fronted box drinking in the vista.

Side elevations

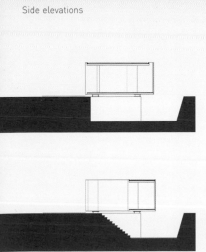

Plan

Front elevation

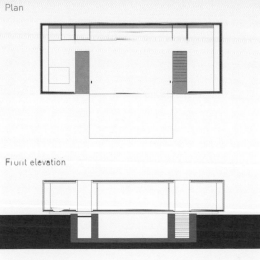

Above At night, the house assumes a new power as a kind of illuminated light box. The open-plan main living room is concentrated at the front of the building, with a galley kitchen and services to the rear behind a metallic mesh curtain.

Opposite The main level of the building sits above a sunken courtyard and garaging at basement level, approached from an access driveway to the rear. Steps lead up from below into the main body of the house.

Above The fluid nature of the house is underlined by the sliding metallic curtain, which separates the galley kitchen at the rear of the house from the open-plan living- and dining room to the front. A series of skylights bring added sunlight into the kitchen.

Opposite In the master bedroom, a bath is hidden away beneath the bed, while a small ablutions area is positioned to the rear. To one side, a light well reaching down to the basement area also helps to divide the wing from the rest of the house.

The same might be said of Casa M-Lidia nearby, although the house has added interest that comes from the fact that it was conceived and built on a relatively modest budget; a contrast, perhaps, to some of the more upscale projects featured elsewhere in this book. The house was built for a young couple who hoped to build on a small plot of land in the foothills, surrounded by more traditional pitched-roofed houses, but with a strong aspect. To keep costs down, much of the building was prefabricated and then assembled on site.

The house is approached from an access road to the rear, leading to a semi-submerged courtyard and garaging at basement level, with the main body of the house sitting level with the front garden. Two stairways rise from either side of the garage up to the living spaces above, and form glass-encased light boxes that help bring sunlight into the building. These stairwells also act as lightly conceived dividers that help separate the structure into three zones, with a central living section plus a bedroom in one wing and a study in the other. This sense of spatial separation in the house is highly fluid and flexible, and a long metallic curtain to the rear of the main living area disguises the kitchen; bathroom and services are also tucked away to the back of the house. A bathtub is hidden under the bed in the bedroom to maximize space.

The climate of the region has been carefully considered, and there is plenty of ventilation along with an extendable sunshade canopy, which can form a protective porch over the more exposed front section of the house. With concrete supports framing a construction of sheet steel and glass, Casa M-Lidia is in many ways a simple, minimalist structure, but one conceived with ingenuity, precision, and a respect for its surroundings. Such principles have led the practice to many larger-scale commissions for public buildings, and to the attention of an international audience.

Casa M-Lidia is a simple, minimalist structure, but one conceived with ingenuity, precision, and a respect for its surroundings.

Opposite The stairwell down to the basement entrance also doubles as a light well, bringing sunlight down into the house. The glass walls surrounding the stairs reinforce the sense of light, transparency, and cohesion.

Above and right The simplicity of the structure frames a series of views within and without. Carefully positioned windows, some screened by exterior grills, allow for isolated glimpses of the bucolic landscape beyond.

Its architects describe the house in metaphorical terms as slabs of rock that appear to have splintered and fallen from the surrounding mountains. The house appears from the outside as a cohesive single-storey structure, yet is actually split into three levels.

Studio Archea

GAZZANIGA HOUSE

Gazzaniga, Bergamo

This sculpted home is a radical reinvention of an existing 1970s building, complete with a pivotal indoor swimming pool.

A path of stone slabs leads to the entrance hall of the house, a complex prism that forms a vestibule, complete with doorways and a small internal courtyard. This intriguing, angular structure acts as a focus for the entire house, leading into a large, open-plan living space.

Ground-floor plan

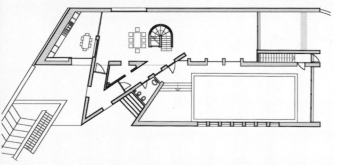

First-floor plan

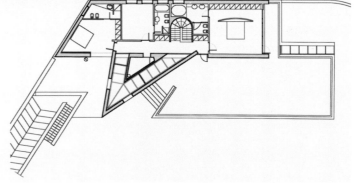

Since its formation in 1998, Studio Archea have taken a decidedly intellectual approach to architecture. The original founders – Laura Andreini, Marco Casamonti, and Giovanni Polazzi – are all university professors of architecture or involved in academic research. From the beginning, Studio Archea has not simply been a commercial practice, but also a centre for research and innovation, emphasizing the use of traditional materials in innovative ways, the strictures of geometry, and the relationship of buildings to site and landscape.

With the Gazzaniga house in Lombardy, then, we have a typically lucid and erudite premise behind the form of the building itself. The house is a radical reinterpretation of a 1970s concrete structure, within a geometrical form explained by the architects as an 'old building shattering into stone splinters, pointed like pieces of rock fallen from the surrounding mountains'. The juxtaposition of clearly pinpointed triangular elements and long horizontal forms gives the house a pure, sculptural quality. Much of the original building was demolished to create the outline of the new house, which is coated in concrete and stone and simply detailed, cut with sequences of vertical windows. At first glance the house appears to hug the site as a single-storey unit, yet is actually over three floors. Garaging and services are located in a subterranean

basement area, while a small first-floor level houses three bedrooms and bathrooms.

Living spaces are concentrated on the ground floor, which is accessed via a complex, double-height prismatic entrance area with a large skylight above, a combination of vestibule and courtyard. Most of the key living spaces connect in one way or another with this dramatic entrance zone, including the large open plan dining- and sitting room, lightly divided by a central stairwell. An additional sitting room looks straight into the indoor pool through internal glazing. The pool itself, bordered with marble, becomes an intrinsic part of the building, projecting outwards from the main body of the house, its flat roof also serving as a roof terrace.

A lack of embellishment pushes the house into minimalism, mitigated perhaps by the complexity of the geometry and the rich texture of the stonework. This quality of raw, masculine simplicity has come to dominate the firm's recent work, as seen in their recreation centre at Curno, in which they used materials chosen for their expressive patina, such as rusting Corten steel plates, perforated to allow pinpoints of light to filter through. Materials like copper, stone, and steel give Studio Archea's buildings a sense of monumentality and weight, but also a richness of tone and texture that further reinforces the impression of a sculptor's sensibility to form.

Far left and left The strict geometry of the house sets up a complex series of intersecting lines and views, with windows cut simply into the building's fabric. Within and without, embellishment is kept to a minimum so that the focus is on materials, light, texture, and line.

Right The large indoor swimming pool is an integral part of the house, with connections through to the principal living spaces on the ground floor. This single-storey, flat-roofed room allows for a roof terrace above.

Opposite An interior view of the apex of the entrance area, with two tall, slim access points to the sides. The glazed roof creates a covered porch that leads to the front doors of the house proper.

With a terrace and balcony to the
front and an internal courtyard at
its heart, this crisp white house
has many of the components
associated with traditional
Mediterranean houses, but
in a fresh, contemporary form.

Jordi Badia

CASA CH
La Garriga, Barcelona

A prototype for stylish modern
living, Casa CH radically updates
the traditional elements of the
Mediterranean home.

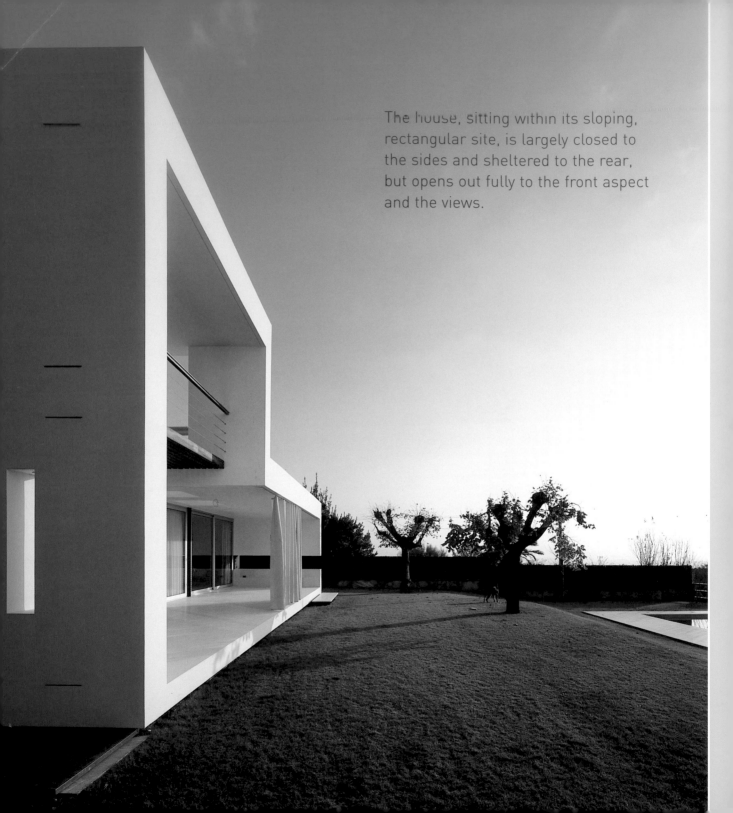

The house, sitting within its sloping, rectangular site, is largely closed to the sides and sheltered to the rear, but opens out fully to the front aspect and the views.

Casa CH takes the idea of a traditional Mediterranean courtyard at the heart of a white building, and applies it to a very contemporary residence. Jordi Badia of BAAS Arquitectes, based in Barcelona, describes the house as a 'matchbox gently dropped on the grass', suggesting the unexpected nature of this radical reinterpretation of Catalonian style.

This family house is located on the fringes of the town of La Garriga, not far from Barcelona and around 15 kilometres from the coast. The rectangular site is long and sloping, with neighbours close by to either side and access roads to the front and rear. The house was eventually positioned at the highest point, with a pool and garaging at the lowest. The main entrance is from the uppermost street, and the unusual frontage of the house faces down the slope. The façade of this irregular two-storey building is dominated by a striking portico within the overall outline of the structure, which allows for a semi-enclosed terrace on the ground floor along with a recessed balcony to the study above. A large curtain allows the easy possibility of shading the terraces and the sliding-glass doors behind, while there is ample room for dining or sitting within the lee of the portico, with its views of the lawns and poolside.

The vast majority of the living space is located on the ground floor, with the large study above

accessed by a striking cantilevered stairway. An ordered sequence of three bedrooms for children and guests is positioned to the rear of the house, while the courtyard, dominated by a lemon tree and planters stocked with lavender, partially divides this series of spaces from the rest of the house. Glass walls and doors to three sides help bring light into the heart of the building, which is otherwise closed to the side elevations to provide privacy. Light is also

Above Located towards the rear of the building, the courtyard acts as a light well and divider, separating three bedrooms from the rest of the living spaces on the ground floor.

introduced by skylights, the stairwell, a glazed
entrance area, and, of course, the bank of glazing
to the front of the house. In addition, there are
other windows and openings that are cleverly
positioned to admit light, yet protect the
occupants from view.

The rest of the ground floor is essentially
divided into three parallel zones, with a large,
long living room at the centre, opening out to
the portico, and the discreet stairway alongside.
To one side of the living room stands the master
bedroom and bathroom, and to the other the

kitchen and utility areas, as well as an indoor
dining room. Timber-panelled walls help soften
the stark white walls and floors, and such texture
is carried through into other parts of the house,
such as the shelving in the study.

Casa CH, then, becomes a highly flexible and
sunlit home - despite the potential issue of
privacy - with constant connections to the
exterior via portico or patio, allowing easy
ventilation and circulation. As such, it forms a
neat prototype of modern Mediterranean living.

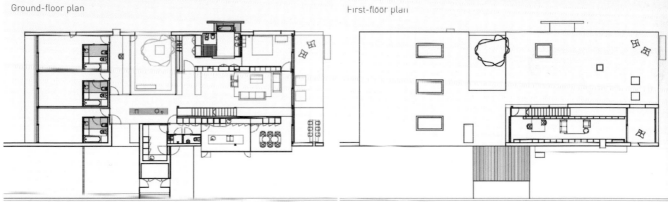

Ground-floor plan

First-floor plan

Opposite The house is largely closed to the side elevations for privacy from neighbours. Yet there are sequences of glazing at low level, along with a projecting light box that allows light into the master bathroom while avoiding any intrusion.

Above Access is at the rear of the house and the uppermost aspect of the gently sloping site. From this perspective, the indention in the wall outline marking the outer boundary of the internal courtyard is apparent.

Right Glass walls allow for a transparent separation between the kitchen and dining area, as well as a view through to the terrace and beyond.

Below A dressing area with built-in cupboards sits to one side of the master suite, which is positioned at the front of the house with direct access to the terrace.

Opposite, above, left and right A series of skylights punctured into the roof of the single-storey areas bring extra light into the living spaces below. The upper storey consists of a large study with its own private balcony.

Opposite, below The house, which the architect likens to a 'matchbox dropped on the grass', is accessed from the rear, where gates and fencing create privacy for the sequence of subsidiary bedrooms.

A view of the central living room, looking back towards the internal courtyard. To one side stands a bank of built-in bookcases, and to the other the cantilevered stairs lead up to the study.

Above, left and right The shower area of the master bathroom features a skylight directly above, while the bath is sunk into the floor within a light well that edges outwards from the side of the building. This projecting box closes the view to neighbouring properties, but creates slim side windows that flood light into the space.

Right From the side elevation, a cut-out in the outline of the house suggests the position of the interior courtyard, which serves as a patio and a major source of light and air.

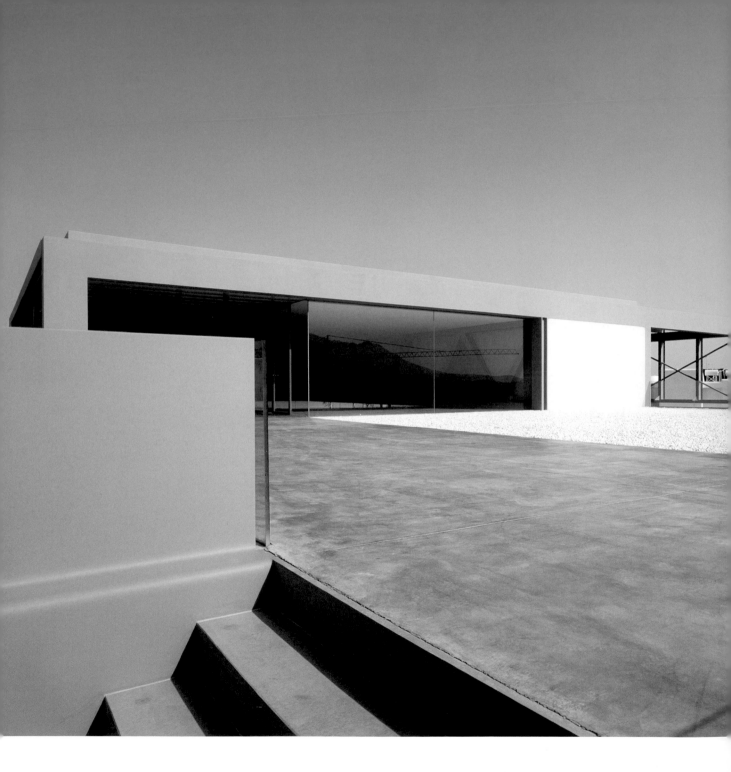

The house is a vast structural object, sitting within a site that benefits from spectacular views; it is oriented to the front on the views to the sea, and to the rear gazes up at the mountains.

Antón Garcia-Abríl

CASA MARTEMAR
Málaga, Andalucía

Strong on imagination and originality, this striking contemporary house shines out among its everyday suburban neighbours.

Antón Garcia-Abríl is not afraid of experimentation. One of a rising generation of young Spanish architects, who counts Alberto Campo Baeza (page 30) and Rafael Moneo among his mentors, Garcia-Abríl has made the most of welcome opportunities to investigate some highly original structural and material solutions in his key commissions for a range of public buildings. Working with an in-house construction division from his Madrid office, the architect has been able to push boundaries and introduce a more versatile approach to building, as well as design.

There is his Music Studies Centre (2000) at Santiago de Compostela, a cube-like, steel-framed structure. Clad in slabs of rough-hewn granite

that give it the appearance of a dense, heavy mass, the building is at the same time well served by light and a spatial richness. Likewise Garcia-Abríl's Concert Hall at Medina del Campo (1999) is coated in a series of horizontal steel scales, which also fit into a game of contrasts between transparency and density, light and shade.

Although not best known for private houses as yet, Garcia-Abríl has taken this love of experiment into a domestic context with Casa Martemar, in Málaga. His client had bought a generous and gently sloping plot, looking out over the sea. But given the heavy development across the coastal region, the site also sat within an increasingly urban context with a variety of building styles nearby. Unsurprisingly, Garcia-Abríl took care to carefully orientate the building towards the sea and to allow for a generous expanse of landscaped gardens and a pool area. Privacy from the neighbours and the road to the rear is provided by stretches of high walls. Yet inside this enclave there evolved a design that was strikingly unique and distinct from any of the surrounding homes and apartment buildings.

Casa Martemar is a highly linear and ordered house, dominated by the extreme contrast on its

Left Structural beams extend beyond the main body of the building to form a long shaded loggia with views down to the sea, a fluid space for outdoor eating and relaxation.

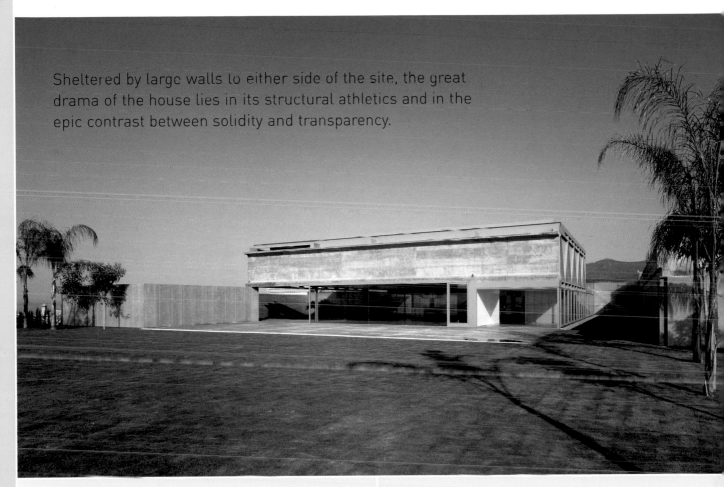

Sheltered by large walls to either side of the site, the great drama of the house lies in its structural athletics and in the epic contrast between solidity and transparency.

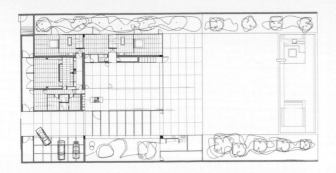

Ground-floor plan

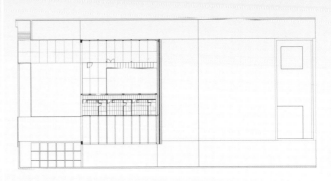

First-floor plan

front elevation between a vast concrete horizontal beam, running the length of the house (25 metres), and the expanse of glazing beneath, which allows for a fluid interchange between the main living spaces within and the terraces without. To the rear of the building there is a corresponding steel beam, while five steel trusses span these two key structural devices and help organize the internal arrangement of the house. The beams also project beyond the outline of the main internal space, creating a shaded terrace and access way to one side.

The house's interiors are minimal in nature, with an open-plan arrangement to much of the main living zones, including the kitchen. A double-height atrium forms the focal point of the house, benefiting from the views out to the Mediterranean, with subsidiary and service spaces upstairs and down feeding off this dramatic hub. Inside, the plays between solidity and transparency continue with, for instance, polished concrete-slab floors and sleek glass balconies and balustrades, which help to clarify the geometry of the building.

Within the faceless urban sprawl of the Costa del Sol, Casa Martemar stands out as an alternative, yet rather discreetly placed, contemporary statement of what can be achieved with a leap of imagination.

Opposite Long banks of glazing and vast glass doors open up the ground floor to swathes of light at one side of the house, while privacy is retained by high walls that surround much of the site.

Above, left The ingenuity of the structural engineering behind the house comes as a surprise, as does its scale. Such methodology might seem more familiar in commercial or public projects.

Above, right The vocabulary used in the range of materials is purposefully limited, while detailing, such as in this shower room, is designed to hide away the workings of the house.

Above The house wears its structural grandeur upon its sleeve, while at the same time presenting a minimal aesthetic in terms of materials and textures, with expanses of glass and polished concrete within the open-plan living space.

Right Elements such as those in the kitchen assume monolithic simplicity within the simple totality of the interior volumes.

Above and right Steps lead to a large terrace on the roof to the rear of the building. The continuing contrast between the solidity of the concrete structure and the transparency of other elements continues with components like balustrades in glass, which allow the eye to pass through and preserve the simple outline of shapes within and without.

A sheltered terrace alongside the pool is formed by a vast awning that also helps protect the communal living spaces beyond. All have views out onto the ocean and of the small island of Tagomago.

Carlos Ferrater

CASA TAGOMAGO

Santa Eulalia de Río, Ibiza

Flexibility is key within this island home, which corresponds in bespoke fashion to the needs of an extended family.

One of the greatest advantages of the Mediterranean home is, or should be, flexibility. Traditionally these are houses with fluid layouts and easy access points between the interior and outside, with a wealth of terraces, loggias, and verandas. The principle of flexibility is one that has been adopted, adapted, and updated within the contemporary Mediterranean house. With second homes, especially, it is important to be able to use a building in many different ways and at different times of the year, depending on the number of family and guests in residence.

Flexibility is the cornerstone of Carlos Ferrater's design for Casa Tagomago, on the northeastern coast of Ibiza and overlooking the small island of Tagomago. This is a single-level home divided into six parts, which can easily be closed down or opened up according to need. A central pavilion contains the key living spaces, along with the master suite, and opens out to terraces and the pool, complete with a dramatic concrete sun canopy, or pergola, which also helps to shade the banks of sliding-glass doors that create a transparent boundary between indoors and out. Beyond this pavilion stands a sequence of four geometric units, one for each of the children in the household. Beyond this sequence lies a separate guest lodge, at one remove from the rest of the house, with its own rooftop sun terrace.

Top A series of accommodation blocks for the children forms a linear progression along the site. Each block has private space of its own and sun terraces.

Above Decking, seating and benches surround the pool and its terrace, which forms one of the most important communal areas of the house, a place for congregating and entertaining.

The concrete pergola forms a key architectural element, helping to frame views from the main pavilion of the house out across the landscape.

Left, above and below A restrained palette of materials – concrete, stone, and timber – helps tie the various elements of the house together and creates a sense of cohesion and simplicity. The building is accessed from the rear, the closed side of the building.

Opposite Landscaping and planting around the house is purposefully minimal, confirming that the house is simply an intervention centred upon its own plot of land, opening up to the existing landscape.

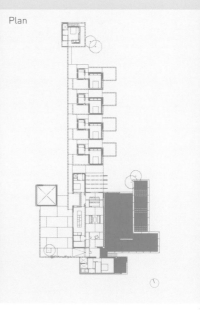

Plan

Terraces and walkways are an essential part of the make-up of the building, offering zones of privacy and neat divisions between the cellular structures that form the house. The territory around the main pavilion and pool is purposefully a more communal area, both outside and in. Typically Ferrater emphasizes the strict geometry of the structure, which sits in rugged grounds of pine and juniper trees that contrast with the crisp simplicity of the house. This simplicity comes not only from the form of the building, but also from the restrained use of a limited palette of materials, both natural and man-made. The use of a sandstone coat over a concrete shell unifies the majority of Casa Tagomago, and sits well with the stone and timber used for many of the terraces and decks. The overall effect is one that veers on the monastic, but also develops the theme of serenity through restraint seen in much of the architecture of the Mediterranean and North Africa. This clifftop house also maximizes its relationship with the sun and sea in its linear orientation, which allows each pavilion its own view and sun terrace.

The principle of flexibility also extends to the possibility of expanding the smaller pavilions upwards, taking into account a future third generation of family members. It is the most elegant of compound structures, able to adapt to many varied demands.

Left An exterior, partially shaded dining area sits to one side of the pool terrace, with benches and tables for communal meeting and eating.

Opposite, above and below The front section of the main pavilion within the complex is dedicated to a semi-open plan living space, with areas for seating and dining. The master suite is located in this pavilion, yet these entertaining spaces also serve for the entire house and for guests, who are housed in another lodge at the farthest end of the site.

Front elevation

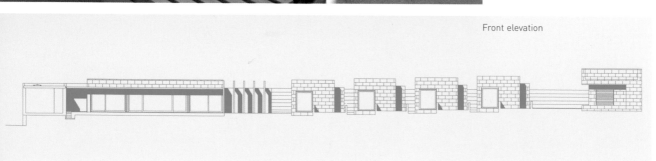

Left, above and below The kitchen and breakfast room are situated to the rear of the main pavilion, which also features the master bedroom as well as service quarters alongside. To the rear of the building, within the kitchen and dining room, glazing is more discreet and is formed of long horizontal strips.

Below Bedrooms throughout the house include private terraces oriented towards sea views and enough space for relaxation. Banks of glazing dissolve the divisions between indoors and out.

The sense of separation
between the interior and
out-of-doors is constantly
challenged and eroded, with
alternative spaces inside
and out for bathing, eating,
and relaxation.

The rooftops of the assembled structures that form the house also provide a series of terraces and seating areas. Bamboo planting softens the geometric lines of the villa.

Studio K.O.

VILLA D.

Marrakech

A subtle reinvention of the traditional Moroccan earthen house, located at the foot of the Atlas mountains.

Morocco has witnessed a marked architectural renaissance in recent years, as well as a highly visible building boom. While many historic townhouses in Marrakech, Fez, and elsewhere have been restored as desirable residences, a new wave of vibrant contemporary architects has been revisiting traditional Moroccan materials and building methods in fresh and original ways.

Native architects like Elie Mouyal and Charles Boccara have helped to reinterpret such traditional materials as *pisé* (sun-baked earth mixed with lime and straw) and *tadelakt* (a stucco-like mix of sand and quicklime). This revival has also been encouraged by foreign architects working in the country, including the American-born Stuart Church and the young French practice Studio K.O., who now have offices in both Paris and Marrakech. Founded by Karl Fournier and Olivier Marty in 2000, Studio K.O. began working in Morocco after being commissioned to design a house near Tangier for the Hermès family. With a number of conversions, restaurants, and houses to their credit in the country, they were then asked to design a contemporary holiday residence in the countryside at the foot of the Atlas mountains.

Villa D. is a dramatic combination of geometric modern lines and traditional Moroccan craftsmanship, with its walls of bricks emerging from the raw ground itself, coated with a layer of smooth *pisé*. A congregation of cube-like structures, the earthen walls of the house are contrasted with other, more contemporary materials, like the concrete of the floors.

'To us there is no conflict between the old and the modern,' says Marty. 'Modernity lies in every element of the past that interests us today. This was our first experience with earth architecture and it enabled us to remain "sincere" in terms of the materials we used for the house, and what appears inside on the walls, also appears outside. It is very ecological and makes the house seem to emerge from the land, while the horizontal lines echo the surrounding farms and the flatness of the immediate scenery.'

Studio K.O.'s French clients wanted a house that was simple, modern, and essentially Moroccan, but was also well proportioned and serviced. The form of the house came to reflect the fact that there were also four children in the family, in that each of them was provided with a distinct bedroom unit, with its own patio and simple, elongated window taking in views across the desert lands in this 6-hectare site. The children share a large, hammam-inspired shower room, while guests are accomodated in two separate blocks at the opposite side of the complex.

The parental suite is set apart and raised up on the first floor, with its large open-plan space

Left and below The house is arranged as a series of structures, forming a compound arrangement reminiscent of traditional farms or modest kasbahs. To one side stand four cube-like bedrooms – one for each of the family's four children – with slim, rectangular windows opening to the mesmeric views. Windows and doors appear as simply cut openings in the earthen walls, which offer an organic foil to the strict, linear formation of the house itself.

Plan

First-floor plan

lightly divided by a metallic screen separating sleeping and bathing areas. Below and beyond lie the main living spaces and a library, while kitchen and utility areas are sectioned off in a separate wing. An unpretentious swimming pool projects out to one side of the house, and there are also a number of patios and outdoor seating areas within the almost labyrinthine formation of the house, reminiscent of the compound form of farms and kasbahs.

The interiors have been kept deliberately minimal in many ways, with little ornament or embellishment, yet the textures and form of the house, as well as that of the landscape within which it calmly sits and communicates, give it a powerful warmth and richness. 'We have been sensitive to the idea of the simplicity of rural Moroccan architecture for many years – farms, peasant houses,' says Marty. 'With its linear shapes and raw materials, it does echo modern architecture surprisingly well, and trying to gather modernity and local traditions in this one building was really the point, focusing on the essential elements: how to provide light while protecting oneself from the heat; how to offer views while staying hidden from the outside; and how to integrate water in a dry land.'

Opposite, above and below
Because the client had a dislike of standard windows, the architects designed a series of openings that allowed light to filter through, but avoided preconceived ideas of standard patterns. Windows, then, might appear as vertical incisions in the fabric of the house.

Right, above A simple, wooden table with banquettes and leather-cushioned chairs dominates the dining room. Suspended lighting illuminates the table, while a bare window above provides natural light.

Right, below In the main living room, a large fireplace provides a warm focus. Walls are earthen inside, with polished concrete floors layered with rugs. Furniture and detailing is kept simple and elemental, in keeping with the Moroccan flavours of the building.

Above, left The staircase to the master bedroom suite is illuminated by a high vertical window, piercing and throwing light onto the textured, earthen walls.

Above, right The courtyard doubles as a partially shaded area, complete with palm trees, for outdoor dining and entertaining.

Left Shaded terraces draw on traditional Moroccan architecture, introducing banquettes for seating areas. The patina of the walls, with everyday cracking and the usual signs of wear, gives the impression that the building is more aged, more characterful, than might be the case if other materials were used.

The walls are constructed of
sun-baked earthen bricks,
mixed with straw and coated
with a layer of *pisé*, a building
method familiar to the region
and which gives the impression
that the building emerges
naturally from the ground.
Here, the complexity of the
project adds a new dimension,
as does its precise structure.
Landscaping is kept to a
minimum, with cacti and palm
trees providing shade for some
of the internal terraces.

Opposite The master suite is on the upper floor, above the main living spaces. A large fireplace and screen divide the sleeping and bathing areas, with windows on three sides. The earthen walls are sealed with olive oil.

Above, left The choice of materials and colours shows restraint, with concrete floors and earthen walls complemented by rugged doorways and simple furniture as seen here, looking into the library.

Above, right The bathtub in the master suite upstairs forms a sleek counterpoint to the rustic flavour of much of the house. Here is one of the very few windows in the house with more traditional dimensions, framing a view of the landscape.

Clad in sheets of Corten steel, the new guest lodge forms a striking contrast to the stone farmhouse. A vaulted addition at basement level links the old and new structures together.

Hidalgo Hartmann

NEW CABANA

Santa Pau, Girona

Λ contemporary addition to a period farmstead breathes fresh life into this idyllic rural bolt-hole.

Left, above Sitting in a secluded location within the volcanic region of the Garrotxa National Park, the original farmstead consisted of a triptych of farmhouse and barns. A structure to the rear of the farmhouse was removed and replaced with the new building.

Left, below The site is not flat, but rather gently undulating. Glazing in the new cabin is carefully positioned to maximize views of the mountains to the rear and down the valley to the front.

First-floor plan

Ground-floor plan

Area plan

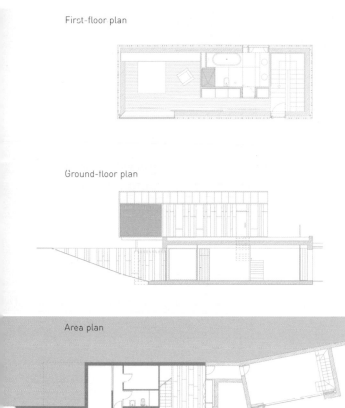

Architects Jordi Hidalgo and Daniela Hartmann make the point that farmsteads evolve over time. A farmhouse might be adapted and extended, a barn added, a stable, perhaps. These changes may take decades, or even centuries, as the buildings adapt to the needs and desires of their successive owners.

Hidalgo Hartmann's steel-coated addition to a small former farmstead at Santa Pau, near Girona, can be seen in the context of this kind of natural evolution. Their new cabin is distinctly modern and determinedly so, creating a strong contrast with the stone farmhouse alongside. Yet at the same time, the building can be seen as a contemporary and sophisticated version of the steel-coated barns and cowsheds that grace many European farms.

This new cabana, for the vacation home of Barcelona-based clients, forms an addition to a period home in a quiet, picturesque area of valleys, hills, and woodland around Garrotxa National Park, a volcanic zone of outstanding natural beauty. The original grouping of structures consisted of the main house, an annexe, and a separate hut or barn within an undulating topographical site. The old annexe was removed from the back of the main house to free up space for the new cabin, and to serve as a linking device bringing all three structures together.

The cut in the topography formed by the removal of the old annexe was used to create an access hall that links the lower-ground floors of the 19th-century farmhouse and the new cabin, as well as leading on to the barn nearby. This stone-flagged hall is enclosed by a vaulted ceiling and glazed access points to either end, which introduce light. The quality of light through this glazing is maximized by the excavation of a grass ramp to one side, where the ground is slightly higher.

The cabin itself is over two floors, the basement floor containing the access from the hallway, plus services and storage spaces. An internal stairway takes one up to the main level, essentially a steel-framed structure resting on the concrete base that forms the basement below. Within this space sits a large bedroom and bathroom, plus storage, creating a self-contained living space or guest lodge. Windows open at one end to the valley, at the other to the mountains.

The upper section of the cabin is clad in sheets of Corten steel, a semi-industrial material now finding its way into residential architecture. The steel plates rust to an earthy, organic copper colour, with its echoes of agricultural sheds on the one hand and a rich textured patina on the other that sits well with the landscape.

The cabana fits within the context of a number of increasingly sophisticated country homes from the Hidalgo Hartmann partnership, and can be seen as an evolution from Casa Masnou, another steel-framed cabin that the practice designed some years before. Both have a simplicity and rusticity, together with modernity, yet create a subtle presence within a grand natural arena.

Opposite and above Sheets of Corten steel give the new cabana echoes of agricultural sheds and silos. The pitch of the roof also pays deference to the rooflines of the existing farmhouse buildings, although in truncated form.

Right, above and below Glazing is positioned according to the orientation of the existing buildings and to frame particular views of the landscape, with windows set flush into the coat of Corten steel.

The reinvented kitchen in the basement, which leads through to the access vault to the new cabin. Renovations to the old farmhouse have created a warm mix of rustic character and modern materials and services.

Opposite The site has been partially excavated to one side of the new basement level access vestibule, creating a grass-coated ramp. This helps introduce light into both of the glazed side elevations of the access area, which connects the farmhouse and cabin and leads through to the third building on the site.

Right The bathroom in the cabin, with a view of the mountains through windows that can be closed with fitted internal shutters. The cabin can function as a self-sufficient guest lodge with bedroom and bathroom on the main floor, and service spaces and storage below.

Located in the highlands of
Mykonos, the house has many
features typical of the island's
traditional architecture, including
the crisp white coat and sculpted
chimney detailing.

Javier Barba

TSIRIGAKIS HOUSE
Mykonos

Rooted in the landscape, this
ecologically-aware home is a
vibrant combination of new and
old, past and present.

Plan

Above High walls in local stone fan out from the heart of the building. These walls help protect both house and terraces from the wind in this exposed position, with its panoramic views across the island and out to sea.

Opposite Stone walls push outwards from some of the bedrooms, which also have their own access to the pivotal terrace and pool area, opening up to the landscape.

Reinterpreting or reinventing the vernacular can lead a contemporary architect in many different directions. Sometimes the references are fleeting, within the use of materials, forms, or colours in decidedly Modernist-inspired buildings. On other occasions, as with Spanish architect Javier Barba's Tsirigakis House on the Greek island of Mykonos, the combination of old and new is much more involved and complex.

Built on a rugged site in the highlands of the island, with sweeping views across the countryside and out to the sea, the house is an evolution of the traditional Mykonian home, complete with crisp white walls and familiar sculpted chimney details. Yet this vacation home for a shipping

magnate and his family also has a contemporary flavour in form, construction, and facilities. Located in an earthquake zone, as well as in a wind-lashed position, the house is largely built on a single level with reinforced concrete walls coated in stucco. But the house is also very much a response to the site and is anchored to it, with exposed rock outcrops pushing into the house itself. A series of walls in local stone fan out from the core of the irregular, organic shape of the house to form a series of windbreaks that shelter the pool and terraces and the building itself, while forming a suitably rugged counterpoint to the crispness of the stucco walls at the heart of the structure.

The main entrance and garaging are to the back of the house, protected by curving stone walls, with kitchen and service areas pushed to the rear. The primary living areas are at the front, with three bedrooms in an offshoot to the southeast. There is further guest accommodation in a modest downstairs level, as well as an outdoor eating area, shaded by a timber awning, near the pool at the front of the building. Interiors follow the combination of new and old, mixing architectural salvage and period furniture with contemporary pieces and materials within rooms that retain a simple, sculpted form.

'The visual integration of the house into the landscape and the way it protects itself from the wind pleases me,' says Barba, whose practice Estudio BC Arquitectos is based in Barcelona. 'Its owners tell me that being so well rooted in the land gives them a feeling of tranquillity, which was one of my objectives.'

As well as being very much rooted in the landscape and sense of place, Barba's work, encompassing houses, hotels, and developments in many parts of the Mediterranean and beyond, is also founded on ecological principles, with the aim of building both sensitively and sustainably. At the same time, he is only interested in one-off solutions for a site, rather than repetitive mass production, which give each and every one of his projects – including Tsirigakis House – a strong sense of individuality.

Right The shutters, white walls, dome, and curves of the building all refer back to traditional Greek architecture, yet these elements are updated within a modern context.

Opposite and below The curved and buttressed stone wall forms a protruding arm that helps to cradle the pool and its terrace. Landscaping is purposefully raw and unobtrusive.

Stone flags and walls, along with
outcrops of virgin rock, contrast with
the crisp white patina that coats
the core of the house.

Left The interiors of the house combine traditional elements and architectural salvage with open-plan spaces and contemporary detailing.

Opposite, above and below The house is built right into the outcrops of rock on the site, which appear to push into the house like lava flows. Here, the stone forms an intrinsic part of the character of the main sitting room, which doubles as an entrance area in an open-plan arrangement.

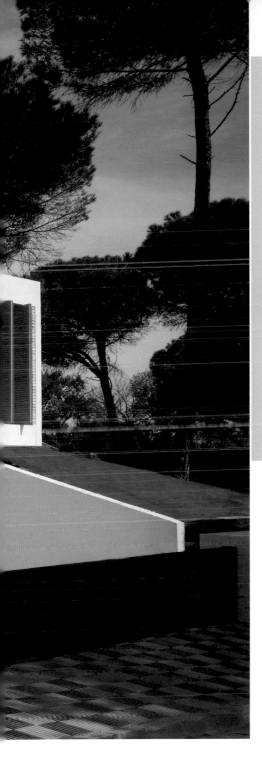

The gentle slope of the elongated site gave the architects the opportunity to create a partial basement level with space for garaging and services.

Catalán Serrat

CASA MJ
Caldes de Malavella, Girona

A new start for a forward-thinking family gave rise to a fresh home that plays with familiar aspects of Mediterranean living.

What we like to call 'contemporary' or 'modern' is usually an evolution, or adaptation, of more traditional patterns of architecture and design, reinvented for today and incorporating new thinking, materials, and technology. In a sense nothing is new, and everything is a development onwards from tradition and heritage. Some architects are more open about this process than others, and are content to credit their sources of inspiration and architectural figureheads.

The young Catalonian practice of Catalán Serrat purposefully build upon their heritage as they develop a portfolio of work that includes homes and government buildings, such as a school in Tarragona. With Casa MJ, their first completed project, Sergi Serrat and Marcos Catalán have been drawn towards some of the natural staples of Catalonian architecture and, to some extent, of Mediterranean architecture as a whole. We have the patio or courtyard, the white-painted walls, the pine-framed windows, and a brise-soleil, or shutter, sequence. They see these staples within the context and example of the work of such Catalonian Modernists as José Antonio Coderch, Josep Lluís Sert, and Antonio Bonet Castellana, so that the vocabulary of the design is clearly fixed within a Modernist framework.

The freshness and vitality of Casa MJ suggest the rich merit of such grounding, as well as the importance of both conscientious attention to detail and sophisticated simplicity. Catalán Serrat's clients sold their flat in Badalona, Barcelona's close neighbour, and bought a site at Caldes de Malavella, a village near Girona and about 8 kilometres from the sea. The site was long and slim and largely flat, but with a drop at one side down to an access street, while pine trees populated the locale. The clients asked for a new family home with enough room for their three grown-up daughters when they visited, within spaces that could be sectioned off from the rest of the house when not in use.

Plan

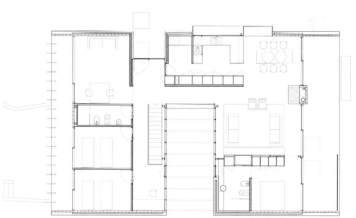

Above The rear of the house faces east and is the most open aspect of the building. Key living spaces open out onto a sheltered veranda and a modest deck, while sliding-glass doors allow easy transition between the outside and indoors.

Opposite The flanks of the house to the north and south are largely closed for reasons of privacy. Yet to one side there is a substantial patio recessed into the building, which helps bring light deep into the structure.

Banks of pine trees soften the site and help provide shade and a natural backdrop for the house, whose low-slung form sits discreetly within the landscape.

The architects used the drop to one side of the site to create an access to a basement garage and service area. The bulk of Casa MJ was then designed on the one floor, with a large patio cut into the house from the southern flank of the building to provide a light source, an extension of the garden, and a natural division between the daughters' rooms to the front of the building and the rest of the house to the rear. These rooms can open up to the west and to a small balcony, with both offered protection by a long brise-soleil of louvred wenge shutters.

The house opens out into a more open-plan arrangement to the rear, or eastern, aspect, with living room, dining area, and kitchen grouped together and opening out onto a terrace with pine trees beyond, while the master bedroom is set apart and to one side. The design of the building cleverly balances the need for privacy and isolation with the need for light and openness to the grounds by opening up to the east and west, but presenting a more closed face to the north and south where the neighbouring houses are more in evidence. This closure is more than compensated for by the patio, which draws extra light into the heart of the house.

To some degree Casa MJ can be read as an evolution of the Miesian box or as a step on from the traditional Catalonian dwelling. Read on its own terms, the house is an elegant and expertly executed debut.

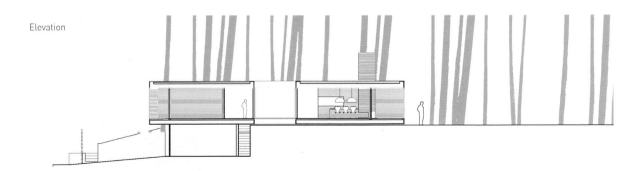

Elevation

A brise-soleil of timber shutters forms a flexible, protective coating at the front of the house, sheltering a slim balcony and the triptych of bedrooms beyond.

Above and right The main living space, towards the rear of the building, is a largely open-plan area with room for dining alongside. Behind the feature wall lies the master bedroom. The space is fed with light from glazing to the back of the house and from the banks of glass that border the recessed patio at the centre of the building, which help to push the garden right into the home.

Left Access stairs lead down to the basement level, which contains garaging and space for storage and services. The three bedrooms to the front of the building feed off one side, while the recessed patio throws light in from the other. A small study area has been slotted in at the far end of the hallway.

Right The kitchen partially encloses itself with banks of cupboards and work units, yet allows a connection with the dining area beyond and views out into the pine trees. Materials such as the white brick for the walls and the white ceramic tiles help tie the spaces together.

Above and right The dining area to one side of the open-plan living space, with side windows bringing in additional light. A fireplace in the same white brick as the walls provides a focal point for this part of the house, and backs onto the veranda. The design of the kitchen allows it to be unobtrusive yet easily accessible, with sight connections through to the main living area.

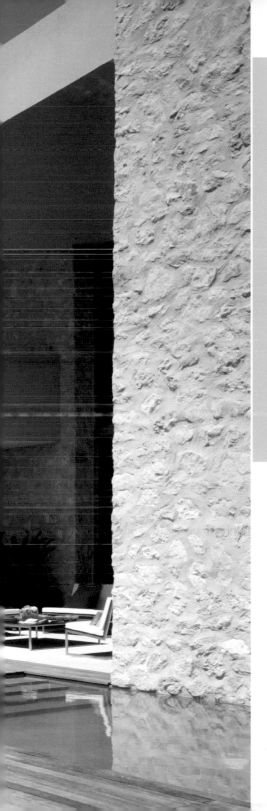

High limestone walls shelter the house from the roadway beyond, while the garden, despite its modest size, has space for a pool and greenery, as well as a gym and pool room to one side.

Ramón Esteve

L'ALCÚDIA HOUSE

L'Alcúdia de Crespins, València

Set around a courtyard garden, this new home has both privacy and character despite its suburban context.

Ramón Esteve is not simply an architect, but also an accomplished furniture designer. His buildings appear all the more cohesive for the fact that he often designs spaces in their entirety, from the ground upwards and from the dinner table to the sun loungers on the terrace. Esteve's best-known house to date, Na Xemena, on Ibiza, was commissioned by furniture impresario José Gandia, of Gandia Blasco, for whom Esteve has designed a number of furniture lines, including one inspired by Na Xemena itself.

This comprehensive approach might also help to explain the elegant sense of order and calm within the family house at L'Alcúdia de Crespins, a small town between Alicante and València, where Esteve's own office is based. Here again Esteve has overseen almost every detail, and has produced a home that stands out both in its contemporary spirit and in its originality within the context of its many standard suburban neighbours.

The modest and irregular site was dominated by an old grain store and other crumbling agricultural buildings, which were removed to make way for the new home. Much of the design evolved around the need to create a sense of privacy and isolation, despite the closeness of neighbours and the curving access road alongside. Esteve created a modern version of the familiar Mediterranean courtyard garden,

bordered by high stone walls and elements of the house itself, which is divided into two parts with the main body to one side and a subservient, smaller building containing a gym and services across the courtyard. 'Our clients wanted to convert this lost site into a new home, and to give the house a rural character within this urban context,' says Esteve. 'They really wanted a space that was inspiring, tranquil, and calm, despite the urban surroundings.'

The courtyard, complete with pool, certainly offers this sense of solitude, while at the same time forming a pivotal space around which the

Left A walkway at first-floor level runs across the double-height sitting room below, and connects the bedrooms and bathrooms to either side. It also forms a striking viewing platform, looking through the portico and out into the garden.

Opposite From the exterior, the house appears largely closed and private, with slim openings in the high stone walls. The entrance door leads into the covered terrace.

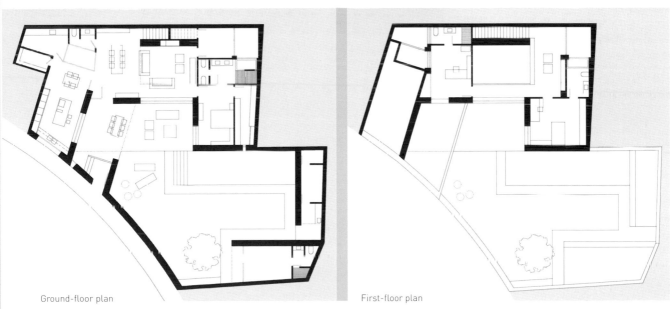

Ground-floor plan

First-floor plan

house circulates. A large covered terrace forms a halfway point between house and garden, with space enough for both eating and seating, while also doubling at one end as an entrance area to the house itself. This leads into a double-height sitting room, vaulted at first level by a slim access bridge connecting bedrooms on either side of the house. Downstairs, the kitchen, dining room, and service areas sit to one side of the main living room, in a semi-open-plan layout, while private spaces, including a study and master bedroom, sit to the other. Upstairs there are a further three bedrooms.

Local building codes and the desire to draw upon traditional materials led Esteve to use a restrained palette of materials, with many of the most visible walls in local limestone, plus roughcast plaster for other surfaces, including the terrace portico. This rough, textured stonework creates both that sense of rustic character, seen to some extent in Esteve's other country houses, and a neat foil to the modernity of the internal spaces. As well as furniture, Esteve has also designed cafés, hospitals, and shops. Yet homes like L'Alcúdia House continue to dominate the attention of his admirers.

Opposite, left A view of the walkway from below, where volumetric contrasts between single- and double-height spaces combine with a fluid layout.

Opposite, right The internal dining space stands to one side of the seating area within an open-floor plan. Furniture is all by the architect, Ramón Esteve.

Above The pool receives partial shelter from both the stone walls of the house itself and the pool room at the far end. Timber decks help to frame the water.

Left The large covered terrace has space enough for an outdoor seating area and dining space, as well as an entrance zone to one side with a balcony above, feeding off one of the bedrooms upstairs.

Opposite As architect and interior- and furniture-designer, Esteve's influence pushes deeper than that of many designers, with an eye for detail and cohesion covering all areas of the house, including the bathrooms.

Slim window openings in the
kitchen-cum-breakfast-room form
one of the few connections with
the street outside.

The house operates on three levels, with garaging in a basement section, subsumed by the banks of the hillside, and a studio on the top level. Most of the accommodation and living spaces are concentrated in the long, rectangular run that forms the ground floor.

Josep Boncomple

L'EMPORDA HOUSE

Garrigas, Alt Emporda

A contemporary and sensitively designed belvedere, this new country house opens itself up to the landscape.

There is a new breed of contemporary country houses in which sensitivity is key: sensitivity to the landscape, to the surroundings, and to the local vernacular. These are buildings that seek to work with nature rather than fighting against it, aiming for a direct and positive relationship with their location and utilizing local materials. They owe more to the natural simplicity of farm buildings and belvederes than to traditional country estate houses. At the same time, they are also distinctly modern, working within a Modernist vocabulary of form and function.

All of this is true of the vacation house Josep Boncompte has designed and built in the rural community of Garrigas, not far from Girona and the French borderlands. 'The original inspiration for the design was the landscape itself,' says Boncompte. 'We tried to maintain the original topography as much as possible, and used materials that could be left in their natural state. Our clients wanted a house that would integrate and interact with its surroundings.'

The site consisted of a series of fields with sloping gradients between them, as well as pine- and oak woodlands to the rear. Boncompte pushed two concrete boxes into the uppermost slope, forming a basement area that houses garaging, services, and a spare bedroom, and the main floor of the house above. Above this was added a striking wooden box, a pine-clad studio that forms a viewing platform or belvedere in itself, looking out across the landscape spread in front of the house.

The main floor of the house is designed to maximize the sense of connection to the outdoors. Essentially a run of spaces along

Above A slim pool and decking run parallel to the main house and to the long pergola, creating a series of parallel lines with shifts in materials, from gravel-coated terraces, to timber decks, to the pool itself.

Opposite The house is pushed into the hillside and framed by woodland to the rear. The branches of the trees will be allowed to grow towards the house, further softening the outline of the building.

Elevations

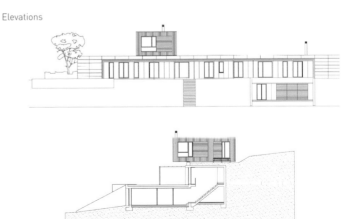

a long, slim rectangular pattern, the four bedrooms are separated by areas for dining, relaxing, and cooking, with a long access corridor to the rear of the building. All of these spaces have their own direct connections with the outside, with doors opening onto a long veranda or pergola that forms a light, cane-roofed sunscreen, protecting the main living areas of the building.

Materials are raw and rustic, representing a contemporary take on traditional ideas. The stone-filled gabions that form retaining walls at either end of the house echo local dry-stone walling. The belvedere box has touches of the agricultural shed or barn about it, while the slim swimming pool, linked to the house by timber decks, recalls an agricultural cistern, with its outer walls lined with local stone.

Planting and landscaping has been planned to lessen the impact of the building on the site, with the treeline behind the house preserved as much as possible so that the branches will eventually overhang the building and provide further shade. The terraces have been reseeded with wild meadow grasses on the lower elevations, and with shorter varieties closer to the house itself. With no other houses in sight and woodland all around, the house becomes an isolated escape, yet one which shows a marked respect for this inspirational setting.

Basement plan

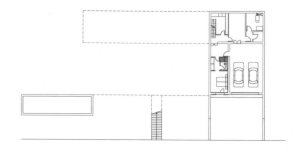

Ground-floor plan

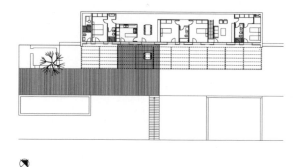

First-floor plan

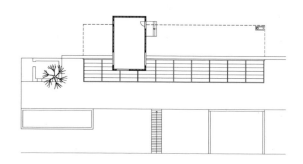

The timber box at the summit
of the house forms both studio
and viewing platform, with a large
window open to the unfolding
landscape. Its wooden form
echoes the construction of barns
and agricultural buildings.

Opposite Most of the living spaces, bedrooms, and bathrooms are concentrated on the ground floor. An access hallway runs to the back of the long, rectangular building, while four bedrooms sandwich a sitting room to one end and a dining area and kitchen to the other. All of the principal rooms open directly onto the terrace. The kitchen itself is partially screened from the dining space by an internal window.

Right The long, cane-covered veranda, resembling a lightly constructed pergola, helps to shade the front of the house. Decking continues in from the pool terrace at the point closest to the kitchen, where an outdoor dining table is positioned.

The original house on the site had all but collapsed, with only the perimeter walls remaining intact. Its reinvention and reconstruction has resulted in the remodelling of the exteriors, and the creation of a new apartment within a large former grain attic to one side of the building.

Joan Pons

DARMÓS HOUSE

Darmós, Tarragona

A new house, full of character and drama, arose from an old, 18th-century building in this small Spanish hamlet.

Right A modest outdoor terrace and balcony sit to one side of the living room and kitchen, accessed via sliding-glass doors that open the apartment up to the views, light, and air.

Below The overall outline of the building becomes clear when viewed from below, as does its context within the small hilltop village. Given the sensitive restoration and reuse of local materials, the house blends in well with its neighbours.

There is a place for contemporary design even within the most traditional of Mediterranean communities. That's the message one takes from Joan Pons's radical reinvention of a period building in the hamlet of Darmós, a small village of around a hundred people within a conglomeration of stone-built houses, sitting on a hillside overlooking a valley and surrounded by vineyards and pine forests, with the Dels Ports National Park off in the distance. Here, the Ebro River finds its way to the nearby coastline, with Tarragona around 40 kilometres to the northeast.

On the edge of the hamlet, Pons's clients, a Barcelona-based jewelry designer and her partner, found a building in poor condition pushed into the hillside, partly collapsed, but with clear potential for reconstruction as a vacation and weekend home. The roof and floors had caved in, although the stone walls forming the perimeter had largely survived, being a good 50 centimetres thick.

Pons describes the project, given the scale of reconstruction and engineering required, as building a new house within the old, with a total reinvention of all internal spaces, the roofline, and much of the façade, as well as the approaches to the house where the driveway winds upwards to meet the garaging and entrance. Yet at the same time, the restoration of some of the perimeter walls and the use of sympathetic materials, which lend the house so much of its rustic character, mean that the house does not jar with its neighbours, and sits well within the context of the village's architecture.

Attic-floor plan

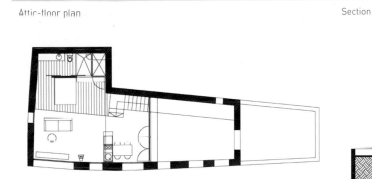

Section

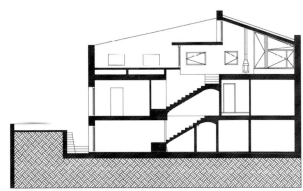

The winding approaches to the house were remodelled and rebuilt, while a garage was introduced at ground-floor level with internal access stairs to the apartment above. The house is perfectly positioned to take advantage of the views over the Ebro valley.

Here we see the first stage of the rebuilding project: a self-sufficient apartment created for Pons's clients from a section of this large building that used to function as a grain warehouse. After structurally resupporting and reconstructing the exteriors of the whole house, including garages, access points, and service spaces at ground-floor level, Pons designed the apartment to make the most of the views across the landscape and to provide both light and outdoor terraces.

The first-floor living spaces were conceived as open-plan areas, with polished concrete floors and ample glazing, plus access to a covered terrace and small garden. The kitchen and dining areas are placed to one end, with a double-height living room to the other, complete with light well and miniature patio to the rear. A steel staircase leads to the sleeping quarters and bathroom above, with an additional roof terrace alongside. The stairs also link to a raised walkway that is suspended above the living room and forms a viewing platform out across the countryside.

So complete was the resurrection of the building that it now assumes a contemporary flavour, with distinctly modern interiors, yet continues to be both deeply sympathetic to and in keeping with its neighbours. With imagination and respect for communal heritage, pastiche has been avoided and a new, contemporary usage found for an endangered structure.

Above The former grain attic has been partially separated into two floors, while retaining a double-height sitting room. A bridge at first-floor level, spanning the sitting room, forms an internal viewing platform and opens out onto a balcony.

Left, above The uppermost section of the apartment, with its own roof terrace. A fixed timber awning provides some shade for the main bedroom at the height of the day.

Left, below Access stairs from the basement garage push up through the polished concrete floors and into the open-plan sitting room and dining area. The organic colours tie in with the rustic flavour of the building.

Exposed beams reinforce the rural tone of the apartment, and pay homage to its past as an attic grain store. Textures and subtle shifts in colour stand out within the overall simplicity of the interiors.

The new house sits on the site of a former forge and blacksmith's house. Some of the existing stonework was used to rebuild or repair the perimeter walls, while the main body of the house is in timber over a steel frame.

Arturo Frediani

GARRIGA-POCH HOUSE

Lles de Cerdanya, Lleida

Within a sensitive site at the heart of a historic village, this new home balances vernacular influences with modern design.

Building a home in the Mediterranean countryside offers its own considerations and challenges as its architect responds to the landscape and locality. Yet designing a new home in a historic medieval village, a tightknit community in a sequence of ancient winding streets, demands a particularly sensitive approach to context and mores. When asked to create a house right at the heart of the old village of Lles de Cerdanya, in the Catalan Pyrenees, Arturo Frediani was required to work within the boundaries of local planning restrictions, as well as within the relatively tight confines of the plot itself.

The resulting contemporary building manages to avoid pastiche or reproduction, while exhibiting real sensitivity to both its surroundings and planning limitations that demanded that the exterior materials be limited to wood, stone, and tiles. 'The historic centre of the village goes back to the 10th century, and both the Romanesque layout and the medieval architecture are protected by strict regulations,' says Frediani, who has headed his own practice, christened AKME, since 1995. 'But this weekend house, located right in the historic centre, tries to suggest new ways of dealing with urban growth, while complying with each and every regulation. We wanted to see how flexible the planning laws might be, and to seek out a degree of independence on the margins.'

The site was acquired by Frediani's clients, Xavier Garriga and Conxita Poch, who wanted to build a second home in the hamlet. Providentially, Frediani already knew the village and the building plot, which included the remains of an old, stone-walled forge and blacksmith's house. Frediani decided to recycle as much of this stone as he could. A few surviving walls were retained, restored, and incorporated into the new building, while other stone was reused in boundary walls and various elements of the build. Even the stone lintel of the blacksmith's house, dated 1801, was recycled as part of a hearth for the fireplace.

The new elements of the structure consist largely of timber, which also features strongly in the traditional vernacular buildings of the region,

Right and opposite The house, clad in Douglas Fir, consists of two units that wrap around the plot until they meet at the centre of the site in a narrow connecting neck. These units can operate together or independently, both having their own staircases, with the larger of the two thrusting outwards at first-floor level to create a cantilevered section with a sheltered entrance area below.

Ground-floor plan

First-floor plan

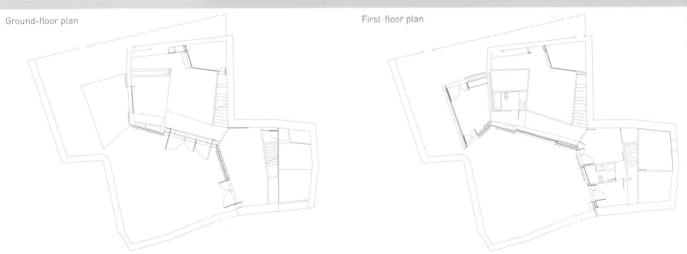

around a steel frame. The exterior of the building is clad in Douglas Fir from sustainable sources, with a good deal of cultivated Finnish pine for the interiors. A sequence of complementary wooden shutters was also designed for the exterior, recessing flush into the façade of the building and hiding the glazing when the owners are absent, thus creating the impression of a closed, all-timber structure.

The structure and outline of the Garriga-Poch house is far from traditional, and naturally lends the building much of its flavour of modernity. The house is actually divided into two parts,

separated by a stone party wall and an entrance passage, and these two parts are also capable of operating independently should the owners require. The larger, dominant unit folds gently around the site, the garden cradled in its lee, with a cantilevered section to one end of the first floor creating a protective shelter for the entrance passage below. The interiors continue the process of spatial contrast and exploration, with shifting volumes and ceiling heights. The house as a whole has been widely admired for Frediani's imaginative response to the challenges and restrictions contained within the site itself.

Right and opposite The house has timber shutters that can be used to close down the vacation house in winter or when it is not in use. These shutters coat the windows entirely and sit flush into the exterior of the building, so that the house becomes a sculpted timber object.

Left Parts of the stonework of the original house and forge have been recycled and used in the perimeter walls, which also feed into the house and add character to the interiors, such as the main living room.

Above A walkway crosses the double-height sitting room at first-floor level in the larger unit of the house. Other rooms and the staircase wrap around this focal point, just as the house itself follows the unusual shape of the site.

Left, above and below
Bedrooms and bathrooms at first-floor level are of unusual dimensions, according to the complex structure of the house. This methodology is carried through to the windows, so that true right angles become a minority.

Irregularity is key within an irregular site. The angularity of the plot and building lends itself to a series of internal spaces of varying volumes and spatial possibilities. Here we look towards the narrow pivot, which separates the two distinct units that form the house.

All key living spaces within the house open out to the front terrace, with its timber decking at the same level as the floors within. When the glass doors are pulled back, therefore, there is an almost seamless transition between interior and exterior.

Rudy Ricciotti

VILLA SEUX BOS
La Cadière d'Azur, Var

In a secluded, bucolic location this subtle and sublime home, pushed into the tree line, basks within the open landscape.

There has long been a radical undercurrent to the work of Rudy Ricciotti. His architecture has been placed in the neo-Modernist camp, yet certain projects – such as the Vitrolles Stadium (1994), a dark bunker rising up in the midst of local bauxite mines – have been labelled not just radical but subversive. The truth is that there is certainly a broad range to Ricciotti's work and a willingness to experiment and hunt for originality.

Born in Algeria and raised in the Camargue, Ricciotti's office is now based in Bandol, near Toulon in the south of France. His work has taken him to Paris and across France, but he is best known for his buildings in the southern Mediterranean, from 'Base Nautique', a wooden liner grounded on the beach, to a series of precise, simple, and elegant villas. These are houses that have had to contend with difficult hillside sites, as well as local planning restrictions, particularly in terms of height. They became vibrant slashes of concrete and glass thrust into the slopes, horizontal incisions like Villa Leyprendi (1998), in Toulon, and Villa Goff (2000), on the outskirts of Marseille.

Villa Goff, in particular, built for an art-collecting couple, is shaken up by a veil of French Army camouflage netting, which helps protect the house from the sun in the day and provides a screen of privacy at night, while also allowing views out across the sea from within. Indeed,

Section

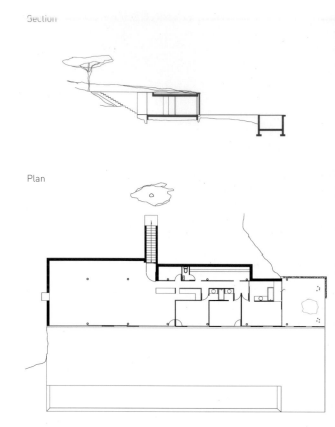

Plan

Opposite Trees pierce the teak decking that flows from the house to the long, slim pool, cut like an irrigation channel. The front of the house can be shaded from the sun by a series of sliding bamboo screens.

Sheet glazing opens the house up to the wooded landscape like a belvedere or viewing gallery, allowing nature to seep right into the house.

Villa Goff shares some similarities with Villa Seux Bos, at La Cadière d'Azur, not far from Bandol and a few kilometres from the sea. Both have steep hillside sites that are bordered with trees, with the houses pushed into the slopes, and wooden decks and slim pools running parallel to the length of the buildings.

Villa Seux Bos, designed for a private client and conceived as a modest single-storey structure, is in a quiet rural spot, surrounded by pine groves with vineyards nearby. The house invites the woods into its environs, with trees emerging from the decking and even winding up through the outline of the building itself, with its amalgam of concrete slabs and steel supports.

All key living spaces, including the bedroom, face outwards to the vista, while a series of sliding bamboo screens help shade the sun along the glass façade, as well as form lightweight surrounds for an integrated, semi-enclosed veranda within the outline of the house.

It is a house that works on its own terms, like Ricciotti's work in general, but also makes an effort to integrate itself into its surroundings. This is helped by the use of such materials as bamboo, timber, and stone retaining walls, all of which help to soften the impact of the concrete and glass. It is, in many ways, a rather subtle building, suggesting that radical thought can be directed into the most sublime of solutions.

Right The divisions between outdoors and in are further confused by a veranda at one end of the house, sitting within the main outline of the building. Glass walls separate this space from the bedroom, while bamboo screens offer shade for the veranda itself.

Within the veranda at one end of the house, trees climb up through the floor and the concrete ceiling, as though the woods themselves were stepping into the house. The tree trunk is echoed by the structural columns that support the building, as though the tree was assisting in their job of work.

sea

The house works on a number of different levels as it progresses downwards towards the sea. The flat roofs of the various levels are simply gravelled, with the addition of cactus gardens on some of the structures.

Bruno Erpicum

CAN HELENA

Balearics

A ziggurat structure pushed into the hillside forms a powerful presence on the coast, with mesmeric views of the water.

The Balearic Islands have been reinventing themselves. Having been a leading mass-market tourist destination in the 1970s and 1980s, the islands have rebranded and remarketed themselves as a more exclusive and culturally aware Mediterranean enclave, drawing in a new wave of investment and a group of more design-conscious architects, developers, and private individuals looking to build homes in the Balearics.

Belgian architect Bruno Erpicum, although based in Brussels, has been working in the Balearics since the late 1980s, when he built

his first house in the area for Belgian clients. Since then, in addition to working much further afield, Erpicum has designed and built many striking contemporary homes in the area for international clients, a contrast to the many pastiche houses still being built on the islands.

Erpicum has developed a sophisticated response to the region, not only in terms of the crisp neo-Modernist style of his buildings, but also in dealing with the climatic conditions, particularly the high humidity, and the need to create buildings that are durable rather than disposable, like much of the older mass development on the islands. At the same time, such houses are also now being used all year round, rather than summers only, and so require better insulation and elements like underfloor heating to cope with the chilled nights of the winter months.

With Can Helena, Erpicum also had to contend with a challenging site, although one which offered a spellbinding vista of the sea spreading out to the horizon. This was a steeply sloping hillside location, with an access road behind and the sea below, and a number of neighbouring properties to either side. 'I quickly understood

Left Bedrooms are situated on one floor, halfway up the ziggurat structure, facing out to the ocean. Each room has a private entrance and opens out onto a sun terrace.

A large swimming pool and sun terrace are situated alongside the
main entertaining areas of the house, the sitting room and the dining
room, both of which open up to the outdoors.

Left From above, one sees the scale of the building and the dramatic slope of the site as it reaches down towards the sea. The house is accessed from the rear and unfolds as one progresses downwards.

Opposite, above and below The house has much of the theatre and comfort one associates with boutique hotels. There is a choice of sun terraces, while various water features help soften the lines of the house and provide focal points as one steps down into the heart of the building.

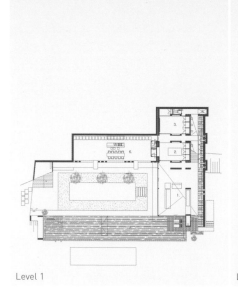

Level 1

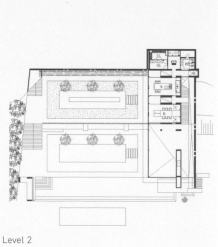

Level 2

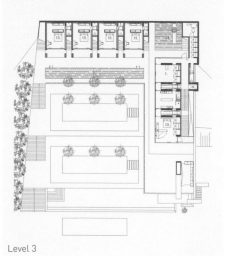

Level 3

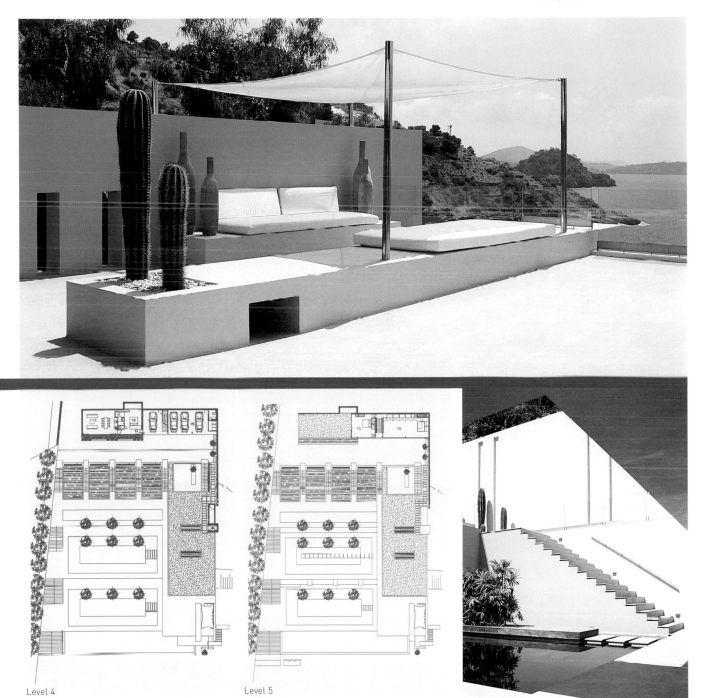

Level 4

Level 5

that the house had to fit into this slope and integrate with its surroundings, yet also avoid any views of the houses next door,' says Erpicum. 'I wanted to design a house that preserved the qualities of the site and made the most of the sea view.'

Erpicum's clients had stayed with friends in one of the architect's earlier homes, and, with one of the family being a designer, wanted an active collaboration in the evolution of the building, particularly the interiors. Erpicum designed their home as essentially a series of terraces, or ziggurats, progressing down the slope, with a large wall to protect the eastern

flank of the building and leaving the western flank protected by trees and vegetation. The terraces naturally face seawards, and graduate over five levels, from service spaces at the top of the site down to the key living spaces at the bottom.

The L-shaped formation of the main enclosure of the house allows for a series of pools and outdoor seating areas in the more sheltered lee of the building. Flat roofs, simply gravelled and planted, maintain the geometric and angular focus of the house, which is served by one large staircase, bathed in light, reaching down into the building, as well as ancillary stairs that feed into a series of four bedrooms, facing directly out to sea midway in the progression of the house.

Inside this house of concrete, steel, and glass, there are also more natural materials, with stone and timber used liberally. Shifting volumes, with double-height living rooms and single-height bedrooms and more utilitarian zones, create a sense of spatial contrast as one travels the house, while key spaces feed out to the terraces and pools. Interior decoration is limited to furniture, artwork, and texture to complement the clean, simple conception of the house anchored firmly to this rocky slope. It is both solid and ordered, yet adapts well to the geography and nature of the location.

Right, above Each of the bedrooms has its own modest veranda; this level is also served by a slim, elongated plunge pool running parallel with the line of the terraces.

Right, below The sitting room is a double-height space, with walls of glass opening out onto the main pool terrace.

Opposite Pinpointed planting softens the terraces as one looks down from the level of the bedrooms and out across to the sea.

The contrast between the smooth concrete retaining walls and the scree slopes behind suggests the difficulties of the site and the inventiveness of the house design.

Above, left and right A water feature along one wall, together with vertical incisions into the structure to introduce light, offset the minimalist nature of the concrete finishes in the sitting room.

Left, above and below The master suite forms a long run of private spaces, including a bathroom and sitting room, which open out onto their own terrace and a view of the sea, both from the bed and from the patio.

Opposite, above A long area for dining and relaxation dissolves the boundaries between indoors and out in the form of a loggia that opens onto the pool terrace.

Opposite, below The kitchen and breakfast room are situated on an intermediate floor between the lowest level of the house and the bedroom zone. The rooms open onto a dedicated sun terrace.

The house is situated on a slim plot, pushed into the rocks. Stone steps lead down from both the entrance and the two guest lodges, which are raised up at the far end of this dramatic site.

Katerina Tsigarida

ANDROS HOUSE
Gavrio, Andros

Perched on a rocky hillside overlooking the Cyclades, this vacation home is seamlessly integrated into the landscape.

Lower-level plan

Upper-level plan

Above From a distance the house appears as a series of stone steps, hugging the hillside and offering dramatic views across the island and out to sea. The traditional stone construction ties the building effortlessly to the landscape and gives it the look of a shepherd's hut or labourer's cottage.

It is a house that arises out of the landscape and its setting, defined by both its contemporary character and by the influence of vernacular architecture. This family summer house on the Greek island of Andros, designed by Katerina Tsigarida, is also a potent and convincing reinterpretation of the Mediterranean vacation home, one that pays due deference to context in every sense, including the needs of its owners.

The site of the house is raw and intense, a rocky hillside plot with views to the east of the port town of Gavrio, and out across the sea to the floating islands of the Cyclades cluster. Responding to the topography, Tsigarida designed the house in a linear strip that hugs the slope of the hill, open to the east and protected to the west by the rising outcrop, with an access road beyond.

Inspired by the island's traditional flat-roofed cellular houses, used by peasant labourers for centuries, Tsigarida decided to split the building into four distinct sections, each made largely from local stone. Two guest lodges form part of this strongly geometric formation and sit slightly above the main terraces and residential spaces, close to the entrance and nearby road. These are simple rooms for sleeping and living, with windows opening to the eastern horizon. A small bathroom and galley kitchen are placed to the more enclosed western aspect of each.

A series of stone steps leads down to the main platform of the structure, with both an open terrace and shaded patios, offering space for outdoor dining. To one side of the terrace sits a service block, with a kitchen and washroom. Opposite stands the largest of the quartet of structures, with an elongated, rectangular open-plan room where the main living area stands at one end, and sleeping quarters at the other, raised up on a stone dais and leading through to a private master bathroom beyond. Here again, the larger windows face east, with smaller openings to the west.

The internal decoration of the buildings is purposefully simple, almost monastic in tone. The walls are bare stone, the floors in metamorphic schist tiles. Ceilings are wooden, with layers of concrete and stone above. Stone benches are built in and other furniture is austere, while wooden shutters are fitted internally.

Viewed from a distance, the house appears as a series of steps climbing up the mountain, the sympathetic stonework creating a natural connection to the surrounding land. For Tsigarida, who trained in Greece and London and worked for Rem Koolhaas's OMA before founding her own practice in Thessaloniki in 1985, it marks a bold reinterpretation of traditional island architecture, combining sensitivity, simplicity, and serenity.

At the centre of the site sits a sequence of terraces and shaded verandas. The verandas, with open views across the hills to the sea, provide separate areas for dining and relaxing.

Right, above and below The shaded outdoor dining space is logically situated next to a utility block holding the kitchen and other services. The main bedroom suite is at the opposite end of the site.

Opposite The house has a commanding position on the rocky hillside, with beaches and inlets down below. It is as much about creating a suitable location from which to drink in the landscape, as it is about creating a place of shelter and pleasure.

Andros House sits within Tsigarida's attempt to re-examine Greek island architecture within the contemporary world.

An outdoor eating area stands to one side of the pool terrace, with views out across the Côte d'Azur and to the sea. The frameless glass balcony erodes the division between house and landscape, allowing the view to flood across the terrace and into the house itself.

Pascal & Francine Goujon

VILLA FLEURIE

Èze-sur-Mer, Monte Carlo

Pop-art influences soften the form of this coastal house of flowers, creating an elegant camouflage.

Above The planting laps at the side of the balcony and is visible through the glass, softening the outline of the pool terrace and adding colour and scent.

As architects, Pascal and Francine Goujon are open to a wide range of influences. They draw on music and art, especially Pop Art of the 1960s and 1970s, as well as a range of architectural influences, including the work of Oscar Niemeyer and Pascal's own father, fellow architect Pierre Goujon. Based in Nice and working together as a practice for the last 20 years, Pascal and Francine Goujon have developed a contemporary approach that sets their work apart from much of the pastiche development along the Côte d'Azur.

The majority of the Goujons' work is now residential, with a particular core of Irish, English, and American, as well as some French, clients, who seek them out to create original homes with a sensitivity to site and scene. This is especially true of Villa Fleurie, the design of which was a very specific response to the hillside site at Èze-sur-Mer, near Monte Carlo, overlooking the sea. The architects found a flower garden on the plot for the house, as well as pine trees and palms, with the hills and cliffs rising up behind.

'That environment was the main guideline,' says Pascal Goujon. 'We thought the villa should aim to be another kind of floral element, rather than a white stucco box. Then we visited the Guggenheim Museum in Bilbao and saw Jeff Koons' gigantic Flower Puppy, and that really sparked the idea of living in a flower house.'

A wall of flowers wraps around the two guestroom suites on the lower floor of the house. The main floor and a pool and terrace are sited above.

The Goujons' Irish client had commissioned the firm before, within a relationship that already stretched back six years. She entered into a full dialogue about the house and its evolving contemporary design, but her requirements were relatively simple, which created a good deal of latitude as the two-storey building emerged. 'Keeping it simple was the big challenge,' says Goujon. 'We wanted to avoid any competition between the house and the views and the light, instead opening up the house to the landscape and letting nature flow in.'

The wall of flowers – geraniums, lantanas, and others – that envelops and camouflages the house wraps around the more enclosed lower level of the building, which holds guest bedrooms plus staff quarters to the rear. Up above, the main level consists of a master suite and a further guest bedroom at the back, together with an entrance area, and then opens out onto a large open-plan space holding kitchen, dining area, and sitting room. Banks of sliding-glass doors take in the sea views and lead through to a large terrace and swimming pool, and glass balconies help to open the house up to the coastal landscape.

Copper cladding wraps around the sides of the building, adding another subtle, semi-organic dimension and tying in well with the floral wall, as it weathers and shifts in tone. 'We are fascinated by the idea that architecture doesn't need to be arrogant to be interesting,' Goujon says, 'and that a building should show some politeness to the landscape. This philosophy threads through all of our work.'

Left The master suite and a guestroom help frame the large open-plan living area on the upper floor of the house, which is pushed into a banking hillside.

Sliding-glass doors maximize the views and dissolve the boundary between interior and exterior.

Upper-floor plan

Lower-floor plan

Above The upstairs bedrooms look
out onto the pool and terrace, and
to the view beyond. The glass slides
back to open the rooms up to the
elements.

Right and below The main living area is an open-plan space, connecting to the terrace. A seating area and dining table are positioned at the front of the room, making the most of the views, while the kitchen is situated to the rear.

The house is accessed at the rear on the upper floor, where a small pebbled border separates the building from the parking point.

Opposite Outdoor dining is possible throughout much of the year, with a canopy of trees providing some shade and further reinforcement of the various connections between the house and the natural world.

Opposite The wall of flowers wrapping the lower level of the building dissolves the line between house and garden. The copper coating to either side of the house on the higher elevations was chosen for its soft, organic flavour.

Above and left The kitchen is a bespoke design with a central island made of black lacquered joinery and a granite worktop.

A Charles Eames lounge chair makes a comfortable viewing point in the sitting room of the house, facing towards the village below and out to the sea.

Set Arquitectes

XSMC HOUSE
Port de la Selva, Alt Emporda

Pushed into the steep hillside above a Spanish coastal town, this family vacation home celebrates its ocean views.

Throughout the Mediterranean, the topography of the region lends beauty, but also challenges. And throughout parts of Spain, France, Italy, Greece, and beyond, especially where the land meets the sea, the terrain can be spectacular, but the difficulties of building a home multiply with the severity of hillside gradients, exposure to the elements, and access problems. Time and again in this book we see contemporary architects adapting to difficult locations, looking to design a building that fits with the terrain itself rather than committing the old hubris of moulding the landscape to their will. Houses are pushed into slopes, terraces created, floor plans shifted, conventions challenged – all with the aim of creating a bespoke home open to the landscape and shaped by its setting.

This is all particularly true of Set Arquitectes' XSMC House, which sits on an extreme site at Port de la Selva, just south of the Franco-Spanish border. The setting is enticing, with views out across the bay and with Cadaques and the Romanesque abbey of Sant Pere de Roda close by. But the topography is certainly challenging, with a dramatic incline down to the village below, graced by tempting beaches spilling out to the ocean. Here, Set's clients asked the firm to design a family vacation home, with space enough for three children, as an alternative to their working life in Barcelona to the south.

'In a setting that is difficult to manage because of the excessive incline, we wanted to design a house that responds to the site's foremost demand, which is to open itself up to the view and to the sea,' says Mateu Barba, one of three partners, along with Josep Carreté and Eduard Montané, at Set Arquitectes, based in Barcelona. 'We created a succession of terraces to model the terrain, including a place to park cars and for building the house itself – areas in which the house ties in with spaces outdoors – down to the bottom of the site, where it is left, sloping impossibly, as a shrub garden.'

Using a steel-and-concrete shell, the architects pushed the building into these terraces, forming an inverted plan for the house. The upper level

Right Painted a crisp white, with balconies reminiscent of nautical decks, the house has echoes of such Modernist classics as Eileen Gray's E-1027.

Opposite The house is accessed from the rear by a slim driveway and parking area within the perimeter of the steeply sloping site. Every possible section of realistically usable space has been colonized.

Elevation

Ground-floor plan

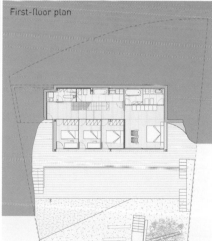

First-floor plan

Above and opposite A kitchen and dining area opens directly onto the balcony on the upper level of the house, making the most of the panorama with trees stretching up towards the house from the hillside. The kitchen units themselves form a partition wall, separating the space from the sitting room alongside.

Left The entrance hall to the rear of the building also features stairs heading down to the lower level, where four bedrooms are situated.

forms the main living spaces, with both the
sitting room and kitchen-cum-breakfast-room
opening out onto balconies via large sliding-glass
doors that can be opened up to the elements and
to views of the sea. Below on the ground floor is
a master bedroom, plus three smaller bedrooms
for the children, again with a balcony and open
vistas. Exterior canopies can be electronically
extended over these balconies to provide shade
in the heat of the midday sun.

To the side of the house there is an exterior
dining terrace, while retaining walls create a

further level below for an additional, larger
decked area. Painted white with decks like an
ocean liner, XSMC House holds some echoes
of Eileen Gray's seminal E-1027, the Modernist
classic in Roquebrune-Cap-Martin, near Nice.
For Set Arquitectes, who build a mix of houses
and public buildings, such as libraries and
schools, in Catalonia and the Balearics, XSMC
House fulfills the engineering and aesthetic
challenges of both the site and of opening itself
up to the seascape panorama.

A modest patio to one side of
the upper level provides an
alternative outdoor eating area
in the lee of the building.

Above and right Decking winds around the base of the house within a terrace supported by retaining walls. Beyond, the garden slopes off dramatically and drops away down to the village and beaches below.

Left and below, left and right
The bedrooms of this vacation house are positioned on the lower floor. Along with the master suite there are three smaller bedrooms for the children or guests, all at the front of the house and with access to the balcony. Bathrooms and utility spaces are pushed to the rear.

Above The garden turns to
sloping scrub beyond the
terracing. From this perspective,
the engineering that anchors
the house to the site can be
fully appreciated.

The centrepiece of the house is a highly flexible living space towards the front, where glass walls can be mechanically retracted into the floor. The room can thus function as an internal space or as a portico open to the elements at the touch of a button.

Marc Barani

VILLA CÔTE d'AZUR

Côte d'Azur

Rich with drama and ingenuity, this ambitious contemporary building reinvents the luxurious vacation villa.

The range of Març Barani's work is striking, even within the region of southern France where the majority of his projects have been focused. They include transport commissions, a water filtration plant, an extension to the Picasso Museum in Antibes, and an addition to the Saint-Pancrace cemetery at Roquebrune-Cap-Martin, as well as the restoration of Le Corbusier's own simple wooden cabin at Roquebrune. With his offices in Nice, Barani is well versed in the architectural history and heritage of the area. In addition, he is responsible for one of the most dramatic villas on the Côte d'Azur.

'It is very rare to have the opportunity to create a grand, contemporary villa here,' says Barani. 'Although with E-1027, Eileen Gray and Jean Badovici really built the very first modern villa at Roquebrune, open to the countryside and aligned with nature, opening the doors to a new kind of holiday residence. That model was then developed in America in houses built by masters of the Modern movement. This project has evolved out of that context and history.'

The family house Barani has designed for private clients is on a far larger scale than most other comparable projects in the area, with six bedrooms and nanny's accommodation, and a generous provision of living space. It respects and follows the lines of the uneven, sloping one-hectare site, raised up on a hillside with views

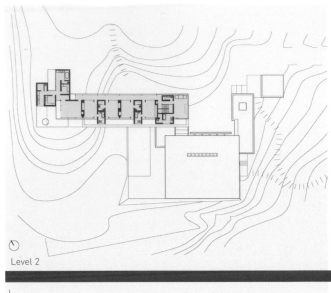
Level 2

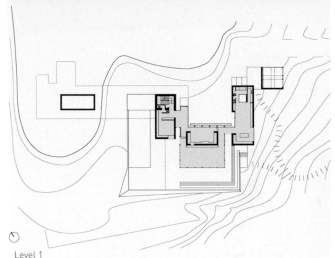
Level 1

Right and below There is a great sense of theatre in the accommodation section of the house, which forms a semi-transparent bridge spanning the contours of the site and offering shade to sections of the pool and other exterior elements. This bridge forms a long belvedere, open to the sea, and holds a generous sequence of bedrooms and bathrooms.

Above One's perception of the house transforms according to the transformation of the living room itself. The visual drama is at its most apparent when the glass walls are retracted and the roofline becomes a vast slab of cantilevered concrete.

to the sea. The epic theatre of the building is invested in two key elements within the design: on the one hand, an intriguing dissolution of borders between inside and out around the main living spaces on the lower floor, and on the other, a clear, linear statement contained in the upper storey 'bridge' that spans the contours of the site and cradles the bedrooms and complementary spaces.

Being raised up to the highest point of the site, this bridge, offering a degree of shade to the patio and a segment of the swimming pool contained in the recess below, offers striking views across the site and out to the sea in the distance from banks of glazing, which help create a notion of semi-transparent weightlessness in this suspended, floating structure.

On the lower level of the building, which spreads out to the west of the site, there is a powerful contrast between great structural slabs of concrete, both anchored into the ground and cantilevered out from the main structure, with the deft fluidity of progression from interior to exterior space. Such divisions literally dissolve as the glass cocoon around the main living room at the front of the building retracts into the floor, allowing smooth progression out onto the patio, with the concrete-slab roof above acting as a vast, gravity-defying canopy. Here the stone floors of the living room and terrace and the surface of the swimming pool all seem to rest on the same level, creating an elegant simplicity of line and a series of reflective trompe-l'oeils in the mirror-like calm of the water.

Working within and beyond the legacy of Eileen Gray, Mies van der Rohe, and Le Corbusier, Barani's villa creates a new kind of prototype for a distinctly glamorous, architecturally progressive style of holiday pleasure zone.

Left and opposite, below The elevated bridge that houses the bedroom block forms a viewing platform open to the panorama. Along with bedrooms, dressing rooms, and bathrooms, there is also a patio and outdoor spa pool at the far reach of the structure, complete with sea views.

Right and opposite A series of glass walls within and without preserves the transparency of the bedroom bridge, served by a long hallway running down the front of the structure. The master suite is situated at the far end of the bridge, furthest from the main body of the house.

The sitting room is a unique
indoor–outdoor room with space
enough for seating and eating, and
motorized glass walls that retract
down flush into recesses in the
floor to create an open loggia.

Right The bridge frames views
of the ocean far below, and forms
a luxurious viewing deck from
which to watch the movement of
the sea traffic across the water.

A rectangular object grounded in
the landscape, the house mixes
concrete and local stone within
a simple structure oriented
towards the sea.

Han Tümertekin

B2 HOUSE
Büykhüsun, Ayvacik

The raw simplicity of the
B2 house and its use of
local materials make it an
apt reinterpretation of the
vernacular.

There has been a gradual but radical rethinking of both the role and aesthetic of the country house. Once upon a time, the country house was a modest, functional, vernacular building at one end of the scale, or a statement of wealth and status at the other. One was almost born of the landscape, using local materials and tectonics, the other tended to be an imposed and alien composition, more concerned with fashion, taste, and grandeur. Now the lines between the two have dissolved, and we have a host of variations on the new country house, drawing upon an extraordinarily wide mix of ideas and reference points that, at their best, are still deeply rooted in a particular sense of place.

The B2 house in Turkey is a particularly interesting case in point. Set on the edge of a small village near Ayvacik, on the north Aegean coast, this winner of the 2004 Aga Khan Award for Architecture is a second home for two

brothers from Istanbul. Yet it is a very unpretentious and sensitively conceived holiday house, built on a modest budget using largely local materials and labour. Designed by Han Tümertekin, an architect based in Istanbul and head of the practice Mimarlar Tasarim, B2 House respects the context of the site in every respect.

Both architect and clients were concerned that the new building would not overly intrude upon the village or its people. The area is rural and rugged in its beauty, with little wide-scale development. There are a small number of holiday homes around the village, but most of the population work in farming of one kind or another and live in traditional houses of local granite.

Tümertekin and his clients, Selman and Suha Bilal, wanted a contemporary home from which they could appreciate and view the landscape, and which would also fit in as much as possible

Section

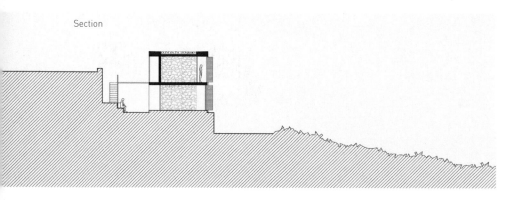

Opposite A series of folding reed panels can be used to shade and close the front façade of this vacation home when not in use, protecting the interiors from the elements in this relatively exposed hilltop site.

with its surroundings. Built onto one of two terraces that are carved into a sloping hillside site, with views of the sea in the distance, the simple rectangular construction was founded upon the idea of framing both the vista and nature. The two-storey house opens up at ground- and first-floor level, with banks of sliding-glass doors and an outer skin of reed panels for shading and added protection, so that the building becomes a frame through which to view the landscape. At the same time, structural concrete perimeter walls to the front and rear surround a thick band of stone at the ends of the house, a pattern that carries over onto the roof. Thus, the man-made materials frame the natural stone, which in turn echoes the familiar materials used in vernacular buildings in the region.

Within, the house is simply structured. The ground floor is essentially one large living space, with a slim kitchenette and service block to the rear, plus entry points. Upstairs there are two bedrooms, with bathrooms again positioned to the rear. Purposefully there is no internal staircase. Instead, an external staircase is raised up on a secondary terrace at the back of the building, winding round to access the bedrooms above, while also sheltering a small covered terrace below.

The B2 house is decidedly raw and modern, sitting in the landscape like a piece of sculpture. Yet it is also of its place, and approved of and accepted by the local community. It owes more to the vernacular farmers' houses of the region than to the look and style of a grand country house. The only echo lies in the idea of the belvedere, a glorious folly framing the vista beyond.

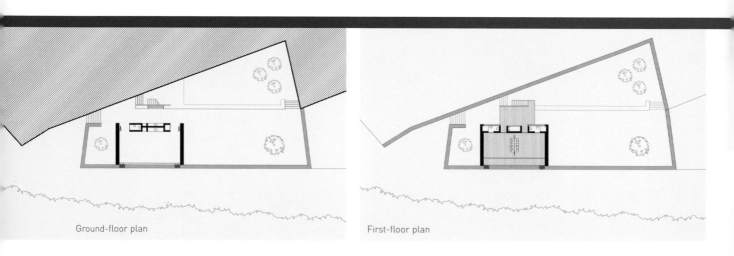

Ground-floor plan

First-floor plan

The downstairs level of the house is essentially one large multi-functional room, with sliding-glass windows that can be opened up to the raw environs. A service block runs across the back of the room holding a galley kitchen.

The rugged outline of the living room frames the panorama beyond.
The kitchenette and services are all contained in a slim bank to the
back of the main living space, with the entrance alongside.

Right As there is no internal staircase to preserve the minimalist purity of the interiors, the bedrooms on the second floor are accessed via an external stairway to the rear, which also offers shade to a small terrace.

White glass coats the uppermost
levels of the house, creating a
crisp shell with a powerful quality
and character that is partly
reflective, partly translucent.

Vicens & Ramos

IBIZA HOUSE

Jesús, Ibiza

A powerful reinvention of
an existing building creates
a dazzling and reflective
holiday home.

Ibiza is an island of reinvention. Throughout the 1980s and 1990s, tourism grew rapidly across this pleasure zone, which sits 95 kilometres off the coast of Spain. It became the isle of entertainment, of clubland, youth, and vitality, blessed with 200 kilometres of coastline, 50 beaches, and 300 sunny days out of the year. More recently, Ibiza has shifted its image to reflect the fact that it also has a strong cultural life and an ever more sophisticated social scene.

The island is increasingly attracting a wealthy design-conscious élite with an interest in contemporary architecture, commissioning architects such as Ramón Esteve (page 130), Carlos Ferrater (page 80), and the team behind the Ibiza house, Vicens & Ramos (see also page 20). Appropriately, this 2005 project involved another process of reinvention: the radical remodelling of an existing house, turning something rather ordinary and unattractive into something extraordinary and enticing. Located near Jesús, a town not far from the island's capital, the house is pushed into a hillside site. The original building somewhat limited the possibilities for the site, yet also provided a challenge that led to some striking results. Working with their clients, the architects achieved a total redesign and rebuild that shows no strains between old and new.

The house now functions on three different levels. The lower ground level is largely invisible, pushed into the hill and coated with a layer of local stone, which is also used for retaining walls and other external features. These stone walls effectively anchor the house to the site, providing a natural link to the landscape, and the floor is primarily devoted to guests and service rooms. This raw, organic stone coat is juxtaposed with the two level structures that sit on top of it, a highly contemporary series of Cubist outlines

Left The crisp artificiality of the glass coat contrasts with the organic tone of the timber deck and other natural features.

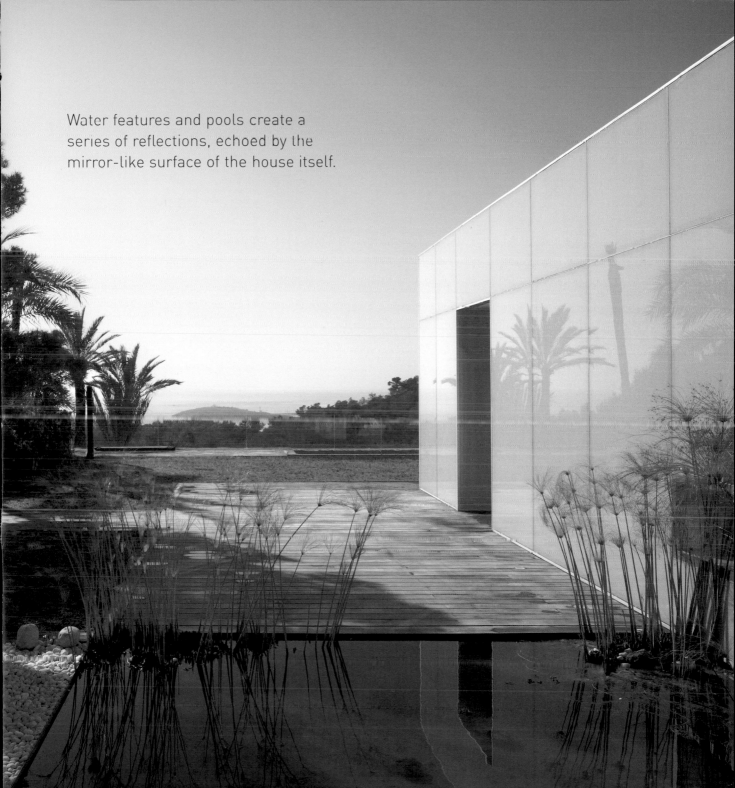

Water features and pools create a series of reflections, echoed by the mirror-like surface of the house itself.

Above and left The house is set into the hillside, with the top portion of the house coated in glass and the lower sections and retaining walls made of local stone. Thus, the building presents a vibrant juxtaposition between translucence and solidity, the natural and the artificial.

clad in white glass, with its own identity and presence. Whereas the stone-clad sections of the house speak of vernacular ideas and the natural world, the glass-coated structure above is a purposefully artificial, man-made presence with a translucent and reflective quality at odds with the solidity of the stone walls beneath.

Indeed, the entire house is a complex artifice with gradations of translucence and transparency as it opens up to the gardens and pool in key areas, particularly the sitting room at the front, which features a portico stretching out into the grounds. The main entertaining spaces are all pushed to the front of the building within a modest upper level, with bedrooms to the rear.

Within the garden, decking surrounds the house and leads to the pool, as well as shooting out in the form of duck boards to connect with elements elsewhere in the landscape. Various water features add an extra dimension, reflecting both the building and the sky. The glass coat of the house also has a reflective quality, forming a soft mirror that offers outlines of trees and sky within a new home which fascinates on countless levels.

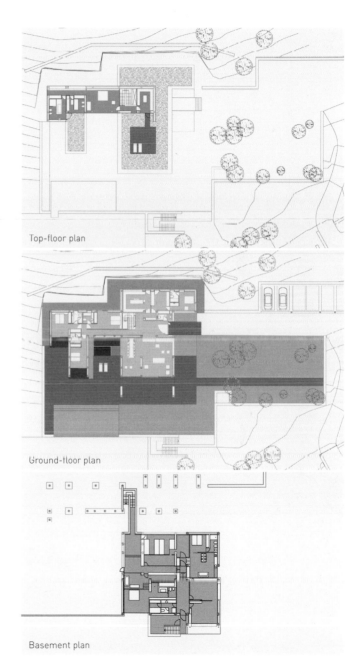

Top-floor plan

Ground-floor plan

Basement plan

Timber decking surrounds the pool and stretches into the garden
to connect with other features, such as the sheltered dining area,
protected by a sun canopy and the shade of the trees.

Above and right The house functions on three levels, with most of the key living spaces on the ground floor and the bedrooms on a modest first-floor level and within a lower ground section. These areas have direct connections to the outdoors.

Right and far right An elegant, sophisticated form of simplicity pervades the interiors, with an emphasis on texture within a restrained palette of materials.

Below Water features and glass tie themselves to sea and sky. The reflective surface of the upper level of the house shifts and changes according to the changing patterns of the sky and clouds.

The key building of Costanza House forms the primary living quarters for an extended family, with space for an indoor pool and a loggia to one side.

Vincenzo Melluso

COSTANZA HOUSE

Sant'Agata di Militello, Sicily

Within an atmospheric and seductive location, a home for two brothers and their families mixes modernity and local mores.

The northwestern coastline of Sicily is a place of intense and relatively unspoilt beauty. To the south, Mount Etna towers over the landscape, a snow-capped, smoking giant, and to the north another volcanic realm, the Aeolian Islands, floats like a small assembly of ships in the sea and has its own active crater in the form of Stromboli, which offers nightly pyrotechnics. It is a place of high natural drama and epic history.

Here on a hillside in a largely agricultural enclave near Capo d'Orlando, architect Vincenzo Melluso has designed a contemporary house that delights in and savours this location. Two brothers commissioned Melluso, who is based in nearby Messina, to create a spacious home for themselves, their families and visiting guests. A long stone-cobbled driveway takes you past a bespoke gatehouse and up to a building that mixes local materials and vernacular elements with striking flourishes of modernity.

'The clients wanted a house that interpreted the contemporary, but also embodied the values of the local building tradition,' says Melluso. 'The philosophy of continuity is one that is important in all my thinking about architecture. The task of an architect is always to interpret and relate the values of tradition with those of the contemporary world.'

With Costanza House, then, we have this striking juxtaposition between local materials and textures, such as the stone that forms parts of the house and boundary walls, or the carob trees in the grounds, and the crisp, white-plastered geometry at the heart of the building. There is a clear framework to the use of these elements, with stone used for all those lower parts of the building in direct contact with the ground itself, while the plastered walls rise above, topped by copper roofs.

Plan

Left The house makes the most of the dramatic views to the north, across the Tyrrhenian Sea, with a series of verandas and terraces.

Below Local stone is used to define sections of the extended building that connect to the ground, including terraces, pathways, verandas, and retaining walls.

The building was essentially structured in
three distinct elements: the main house, a guest
lodge, and the grounds themselves. The house
is arranged in a U-shaped formation, opening
outwards towards the sea with a green courtyard
at its heart. The living quarters sit in two-storey
wings to either side of a lower section, holding
an indoor swimming pool at the centre. The guest
house lies to the east of the main residence, with
an outdoor pool separating the two and stone-
built loggias forming shaded seating areas allied
to both structures.

Within the structural organization of the
house, appreciation of the vista is maximized
with appropriately positioned balconies and
terraces. Landscaping has preserved the native
carob trees and introduced cactus gardens and
ordered grasslands. As with the house itself,
there is a continual contrast between the natural
and the man-made, the formal and the informal,
geometry and texture. Such relationships, along
with the richness of the Sicilian light, help to
bring Costanza House to life.

Right, above and below The main building is a complex
structure, with accommodation to either end and an indoor
swimming pool in the centre. The house folds around a large
courtyard, which opens out to the sea views.

Right and below The house as a whole consists of a number of separate elements that create a compound feeling to the site, echoing small rural communities and farmsteads that also feature a number of buildings in close proximity, from farmhouses and barns to stores.

Opposite The interiors of the main house feature a journey through varying volumes and ceiling heights as the building expands and contracts. Double height voids add drama, but also serve to introduce extra light from above.

Right, above The guest lodge is a separate structure, with a long single elevation, clad in stone and extending outwards to the sea. It holds a pool room, serving the swimming pool alongside, and a long loggia, or *occaso*, connecting to the terrace.

Right, below The house combines classic Mediterranean characteristics: white-painted plaster, raw stone, exotic planting, and sublime views.

Opposite, above The main approach to the house is flanked by an area for underground parking. The landscaping makes use of low retaining walls and stone elements to create a series of terraces, rather like an agricultural system.

Above Carob trees dot the foreground, with the guest house and loggia behind the pool. As elsewhere, low-slung elements, such as the loggia, are coated in local stone.

Right A view from the indoor pool in the main house, across to the carob tree in the centre of the courtyard. The pool becomes a central meeting point between the building's two wings.

The clear waters of the pool give way to the wildness of the landscape and the ocean. Both offer their obvious temptations.

Directory of Architects

JORDI BADIA [62]
BAAS Arquitectes
Avinguda Frederic Rahola, 63
08032 Barcelona
Spain
T 34 93 358 0111
F 34 93 358 0194
E info@jordibadia.com
W www.jordibadia.com

MARC BARANI [214]
Atelier Barani
27, boulevard Joseph Garnier
06000 Nice
France
T 33 4 93 51 08 10
F 33 4 93 51 53 11
E contact@atelierbarani.com

JAVIER BARBA [110]
Estudio BC Arquitectos
Plaça Eguilaz, 10
08017 Barcelona
Spain
T 34 93 204 4206
F 34 93 204 2697
E bcestudio@bcarquitectos.com
W www.bcarquitectos.com

BFP ARCHITECTES [38]
Robin Perna
Carrer de Vallirana, 7
08006 Barcelona
Spain
T 34 93 415 7417
F 34 93 415 5869
E info@perna-arquitectos.com
W www.perna-arquitectos.com

Pablo Beltrán
Carrer de Pau Claris, 173
08037 Barcelona
Spain
T 34 93 487 9341
F 34 93 489 9342
E pablobeltran@coac.net

Alfonso Fernández
Passeig de Sant Joan, 97
08009 Barcelona
Spain
T 34 93 476 5193
F 34 93 476 5170
E alf@coac.es

JOSEP BONCOMPTE [138]
Josep Boncompte
Carrer de Pau Claris, 117
08009 Barcelona
Spain
T 34 93 487 9186
F 34 93 488 2505
E boncompte@coac.net

ALBERTO CAMPO BAEZA [30]
Estudio Arquitectura Campo Baeza
Calle Almirante, 9
28004 Madrid
Spain
T 34 91 701 0695
F 34 91 521 7061
E estudio@campobaeza.com
W www.campobaeza.com

CATALÁN SERRAT [120]
Sergi Serrat, Marcos Catalán
Carrer Ciutat de Granada, 82
08005 Barcelona
Spain
T 34 93 486 9029
E mcs.ssg@gmail.com

BRUNO ERPICUM [172]
Atelier d'Architecture/
Bruno Erpicum & Partenaires
Avenue Reine Astrid, 452
1950 Kraainem
Belgium
T 32 2 687 2717
F 32 2 687 5680
E aabe@erpicum.org
W www.erpicum.org

RAMÓN ESTEVE [130]
Ramón Esteve Estudio de Arquitectura
Callejón de Jorge Juan, 8
46004 València
Spain
T 34 96 351 0434
F 34 96 351 0469
E media@ramonesteve.com
W www.ramonesteve.com

CARLOS FERRATER [80]
Carlos Ferrater
Carrer de Balmes, 145
08008 Barcelona
Spain
T 34 93 238 5136
F 34 93 416 1306
E carlos@ferrater.com
W www.ferrater.com

ARTURO FREDIANI [154]
AKME/A. Frediani Arquitectura
Ctra. de Barcelona, 8
Viladecans 08840 Barcelona
Spain
T 34 93 659 0109
E akme@coac.es

ANTÓN GARCIA-ABRÍL [72]
Ensamble Studio
Calle Cristobal Bordiú, 55
28003 Madrid
Spain
T 34 91 541 0848
F 34 91 553 5004
E administracion@ensamble.info
W www.ensamble.info

PASCAL & FRANCINE GOUJON [192]
P+P+F Goujon Architecte
229, promenade des Anglais
06200 Nice
France
T 33 4 93 71 89 10
F 33 4 93 83 92 97
E pascal@ppfgoujon.net
W www.ppfgoujon.net

HIDALGO HARTMANN [102]
Jordi Hidalgo, Daniela Hartmann
Carrer del Rosselló, 302
08037 Barcelona
Spain
T 34 93 457 6668
E jhidalgo@coac.net

Verge de Núria, 1
Olot 17800 Girona
Spain
T 34 972 264 063

VINCENZO MELLUSO [244]
Melluso Architettura
Riviera Place, 451
98167 Messina
Italy
T/F 39 90 310 981
E into@mellusoarchitettura.it
W www.mellusoarchitettura.it

JOAN PONS [146]
Joan Pons
Carrer de Llull, 47-49
08005 Barcelona
Spain
T 34 93 317 0128

RCR ARQUITECTES [48]
*Rafael Aranda, Carmen Pigem,
Ramón Vilalta*
Passeig de Blay, 34
Olot 17800 Girona
Spain
T 34 972 269 105
F 34 972 272 267
E rcr@rcrarquitectes.es
W www.rcrarquitectes.es

RUDY RICCIOTTI [162]
Agence Rudy Ricciotti Architecte
17, boulevard Victor Hugo
83150 Bandol
France
T 33 4 94 29 52 61
F 33 4 94 32 45 25
E rudy.ricciotti@wanadoo.fr

SET ARQUITECTES [204]
Mateu Barba, Eduard Montané
Carrer de Provença, 293
08037 Barcelona
Spain
T 34 93 207 0611
F 34 93 457 2069
E mateu_barba@coac.net
E e.montane@coac.net

Josep Carreté
Avinguda de Vallvidrera, 69
08017 Barcelona
Spain
T 34 93 418 6447
F 34 93 252 0467
E j.carrete@coac.net

STUDIO ARCHEA [56]
*Laura Andreini, Marco Casamonti, Silvia
Fabi, Gianna Parisse, Giovanni Polazzi*
Lungarno Benvenuto Cellini, 13
50125 Florence
Italy
T 39 55 658 0127
F 39 55 681 0850
E staff@archea.it
W www.archea.it

STUDIO K.O. [92]
Karl Fournier, Olivier Marty
7, rue Geoffroy l'Angevin
75004 Paris
France
T 33 1 42 71 13 92
F 33 1 42 71 13 94
E koparis@studioko.fr
W www.studioko.fr

127, avenue Mohamed V
Marrakech, Morocco
T 212 4 443 7678
F 212 4 443 7632
E komarrakech@studioko.fr

KATERINA TSIGARIDA [184]
Katerina Tsigarida Architects
N. Votsi 3
Limani 54625 Thessaloniki
Greece
T 30 2310 526 563
F 30 2310 535 916
E contact@tsigarida.gr
W www.tsigarida.gr

HAN TÜMERTEKIN [224]
Mimarlar Tasarim Danismanlik Ltd
Cinarli Cesme Sokak Gunluk Cikmazi, 1
Kurucesme 80820 Istanbul
Turkey
T 90 212 358 2760
F 90 212 358 2762
E mimarlar@mimarlar.com
W www.mimarlar.com

VICENS & RAMOS [20, 234]
Ignacio Vicens, José Antonio Ramos
Calle Barquillo, 29
28004 Madrid
Spain
T 34 91 521 0004
F 34 91 532 4842
E vicensramos@arquired.es